THE DILEMMA

DELIVERANCE OR DISCIPLINE?

THE DILEMMA

DELIVERANCE OR DISCIPLINE?

W. Robert McAlister

LOGOS INTERNATIONAL
PLAINFIELD, NEW JERSEY

Unless otherwise noted, all Biblical quotations are from the New American Standard Bible, Carol Stream, Ill.: Creation House, Inc., © 1971

Abbr: KJV — King James version
      TAB — The Amplified Bible, Grand Rapids, Mich.: Zondervan. © 1965.
      RSV — Division of Christian Education of the National Council of Churches of Christ of the United States of America. © 1946, 1952, 1971.

Other translations used:

The New Testament in Modern English, translated by J.B. Phillips, New York: Macmillan. © 1958.

The New Testament from 26 Translations, Grand Rapids, Mich.: Zondervan. © 1967.

The New Testament in Modern Speech, Boston & London, Pilgrim Press. © 1943.

Interlinear Greek-English New Testament with Lexicon and Synonyms, Grand Rapids, Mich.: Zondervan. © 1958.

Printed in the United States of America
Library of Congress Catalog Card Number: 75-38196
ISBN: 0-88270-150-9
Published by Logos International, Plainfield, New Jersey, 07061.

CONTENTS

Foreword

I have no controversy with exorcism of demons in unbelievers, but I must reject the doctrine that says demons could inhabit Christians who are truly born of the Spirit. Recent books and articles which teach this are the most faith-destroying and fear-inspiring perversion of Scripture that I have ever read. I would plead with all readers to consider the admonition of the Word, "As therefore you received Christ Jesus the Lord, so live in him, rooted and built up in him and established in the faith, just as you were taught, abounding in thanksgiving. See to it that no one makes a prey of you by philosophy and empty deceit, according to human tradition, according to the elemental spirits of the universe, and not according to Christ. For in him the whole fulness of deity dwells bodily, and you have come to fulness of life in him, who is the head of all rule and authority" (Col. 2:6-10 RSV).

While recognizing that evil spirits are very real and active, I do not consider all sickness and failure or discouragement to be the product of demon activity. The works of the flesh (Gal. 5:19-21 KJV) and the reprobate mind (Rom. 1:28-32 KJV) are not "little demons" that must come out by exorcism, but rather *sins* that must be confessed and forgiven by the cleansing blood of Jesus (I John 1:7-10). Let us acknowledge our guilt and not blame it on demons.

During fifty years of ministry all over the world, I have seen some of the worst sinners, in all categories of wickedness, confess their sin, accept forgiveness, take a drink of living water from Jesus (John 4:14) and, without any further ado, become satisfied and happy saints. However, this does not mean that there never came an hour of temptation. When Jesus was tempted, He did not have a demon in Him. It was Satan himself who shot his fiery darts of suggestions into His mind, and Jesus quickly quenched them with the shield of faith in His Father's Word (Eph. 6:16-17).

For those who do not yet know the glorious "liberty wherewith Christ hath made us free" (Gal. 5:1 KJV), this book gives us a record of what can be accomplished in the name of Jesus by the power of the Holy Spirit.

Before Jesus died as "the lamb of God that takes away the sin of the world," He Himself delivered, by the power of the Holy Spirit, those who were "oppressed of the devil." However, He died on the cross of Calvary "that through death he might destroy him that had the power of death, that is, the devil" (Heb. 2:14 KJV). We have no record that He cast a devil out of anyone after His resurrection. Rather He breathed on them and said, "Receive ye the Holy Ghost."

Those who have accepted Jesus Christ as their Redeemer have been "delivered . . . from the power of darkness . . . translated . . . into the kingdom of his dear Son: In whom we have redemption through his blood, even the forgiveness of sins" (Col. 1:13-14 KJV). Jesus said, "Dwell in Me and I will dwell in you" (John 15:4 TAB). Thus for those who are born again, it is always: "Christ in you, the hope of glory" (Col. 1:27 KJV). Let us accept the truth. "Ye are of God, little children, and have overcome them: because greater is he that is in you, than he that is in the world" (I John 4:4 KJV).

Let not the children of God seek deliverance by exorcism, but "Let us . . . come boldly unto the throne of grace, that we may obtain mercy, and find grace to help in time of need" (Heb. 4:16 KJV).

David J. duPlessis
Oakland, California

THE DILEMMA

DELIVERANCE OR DISCIPLINE?

Chapter I
WHY ANOTHER BOOK ABOUT DEMONS?

We had just committed Fred's mother to the psychiatric ward of the hospital.

Fred wept, "She just kept on casting the demon of asthma out of me, and I don't even have asthma!" Fewer than two weeks before, Fred's mother had attended a home prayer meeting where she had been given the "ministry of deliverance."

It is for Fred and his mother, and thousands of believers just like them that I was finally persuaded by the Holy Spirit to write this book. I was very reluctant to enter an area so fraught with controversy and confusion. My ministry is dedicated to those truths that bring us as priests into the presence of the Lord and equip us to minister to the Body of Christ and to the unsaved. I do not enjoy the subjects of demonology and exorcism.

Many sincere people of God espouse the theory of demons-in-believers so that I can only ask for the help of the

Holy Spirit to explain in genuine humility what I have learned about demons through hard experience. I hope that we might find and speak the truth, in love, about deliverance, so that people like Fred and his mother will not become obsessed with fears of the spirit world, about which so very little is known.

In the past, the problem of demonism has been confined generally to the mission fields: those countries with a history of paganism or occult religions. This is no longer true. Demon possession has become a universal plague.

Most of the illustrations I will use are drawn from twenty-three years of ministry in the Orient, Europe and Latin America as well as across the United States.

In returning to America for brief periods of time during these years of overseas ministry, I have become aware of the growing manifestation of demonism, and of the great lack of information among God's people about this problem. I am alarmed by the teaching that believers can be demon possessed, and have waited for someone to challenge it.

In talking with pastors and believers in many different parts of the United States, I find that the word "deliverance" (which used to mean healing) has taken on definitions that I cannot justify from a study of the Scriptures. For example, I have recently read books that tell me about demons of gluttony and forgetfulness. What are these demons and why doesn't the Bible talk about them?

Having prayed for the sick on four continents and learned that prayer offered in faith will restore one who is sick (James 5:15), I have met people recently who tell me that virtually all pain and sickness is the consequence of the presence of demons. This does not agree with what I have experienced, nor does it seem to have a Biblical foundation.

In this book I want to make a clear distinction between satanism and demonism. Jesus went about healing all who were "oppressed by the devil" (Acts 10:38). In John 10:10 we find that Satan's work is to steal, to kill and to destroy. But the Bible clearly teaches that the devil can be resisted. "Resist the devil and he will flee from you" (James 4:7).

Demons, on the other hand, possess a body to torment it. If there is no resistance, demons may enter and leave a body at will. "When the unclean spirit goes out of a man, it passes through waterless places seeking rest, and not finding any, it says, 'I will return to my house from which I came' " (Luke 11:24).

The Bible does not tell us to resist demons. The reason is simple. In order for demons to enter and possess a human body, there must exist a climate of evil, created by a willfully sinful life, that makes it impossible to impede demonic entrance.

If the distinction between the devil and demons—between satanic oppression and demonic possession—can be understood, many questions will be answered and problems solved. This difference is not merely one of semantics. It is fundamental. We must know what the Bible teaches about these two areas of evil so that we will be free from fear, and properly equipped to deal with the devices of the devil.

The Thing

Clarita Villenueva was a prostitute who had come to Manila from a province in the interior of the Philippine Islands. Picked up by the police on a charge of vagrancy, she was taken to the infamous Billibid Prison where a few years previously the Japanese had tortured Filipino and American prisoners during the Second World War.

On the first night of her confinement, Clarita awoke screaming in terror. She claimed that two men had bitten her. As proof she showed the guard the marks of teeth on the nape of her neck and the inside of both upper arms. She was examined by Dr. Lara, the prison doctor. The next morning, a curious news reporter heard about it and a Manila paper announced that "The Thing" had bitten a local girl.

The whole matter would probably have been forgotten at that point had not Dr. Lara agreed to demonstrate this strange thing for the prison officials and local newsmen. One of them had a tape recorder at this session and, later that evening, Clarita's screams were broadcast all over the central Philippine Islands.

This happened in the spring of 1952 when I was conducting a series of meetings in Bethel Temple, pastored by the Reverend Lester Sumrall. We listened to that eerie broadcast together.

The next morning, Mr. Sumrall asked me to accompany him to Dr. Lara, who was also chief pathologist for the city of Manila. He arranged for us to visit Clarita.

By this time the story was being carried on international wire services under the sensational headline, "Bitten by The Thing." Consequently, when we entered the dormitory cell of Billibid Prison, we were followed by prison guards and reporters from both local and international news services, as well as a large number of inmates who evidently had the freedom of that part of the prison.

During the moments of introduction, Clarita's appearance was normal in every way, but when Mr. Sumrall seated himself in front of her and reached out his hand in her direction, she became another person. Her eyes dilated and her face took on a look of hatred. Her body stiffened and she flung her arms outward. I saw fresh teeth marks appear on the flat surface of her inner arms and saliva appear where there had been no human mouth.

Between her screams of terror came blasphemous words, spoken in clear English, a language that was almost unknown to this simple girl from a northern province. As her violence increased, both Dr. Lara and the chief of police had to restrain this hundred-pound, teenage girl.

It was a frightening scene. Most of the guards and prisoners were kneeling. Some were praying; others were crying. Reporters tried to keep up with what everybody was saying. During this emotion-packed half hour, I saw the struggle between demonic power and the authority of the name of Jesus.*

This was my first exposure to demon possession, but not the last.

The Legion Of Blood

In 1962 while pastoring the New Life Pentecostal Church in Rio de Janeiro, Brazil, I was asked to visit Astrea who had hemorrhaged daily for over fifteen years. Having exhausted the resources of medical science on three continents, her elderly father came to ask me to pray for her healing.

During my first visit with Astrea, I was told about her strange illness. In daily attacks that lasted up to two hours she bled from the eyes, nose, ears and mouth. I prayed for her healing and declared that, if this strange sickness was caused by demonic power, it be rebuked in the name of Jesus. As soon as I had left the room, Astrea heard a familiar voice say, "The other one is going to leave, but I'm staying."

On my second visit I was told that Astrea was in the

---

*The full story with its happy conclusion is to be found in the book, *The Deliverance of Clarita Villenueva* by Lester F. Sumrall.

17

bathroom in the midst of an attack. When I opened the door I was confronted with a ghastly sight. Blood was dripping from Astrea's ears, oozing from her eyes, and bubbling from between clenched teeth.

I commanded her to speak to me. From deep in her throat came a bass voice telling me that I was in the presence of a demon from the legion of blood. I commanded him to leave in the name of Jesus. He insisted that Astrea's body was his house; that he had every right to be there and, furthermore, he had no intention of leaving after more than fifteen years of residence.

After repeatedly bringing the authority of the name of Jesus against him, the demon left and Astrea stopped bleeding. Then I began to explain to her the facts of demon possession. This was the first time her problem had been properly diagnosed. During the fifteen years of suffering she had been treated for epilepsy, lockjaw, insanity and assorted other maladies.

On two more occasions I confronted this demon as he tried to claim squatter's rights in the body of this cultured, middle-aged Brazilian woman. On each occasion the demon left and Astrea slumped to the floor in complete exhaustion. Twice more I explained about the activity of demons and the power that believers possess through the name of Jesus.

It was a Sunday evening when the final confrontation almost took Astrea's life. I was called to come quickly because Astrea had locked herself in the bathroom; something she never did due to the frequency of the attacks. Blood had begun to seep under the door and the family could get no response to their cries. They were afraid that Astrea had already died. Before calling a taxi to rush me to their penthouse apartment on Rio's Copacabana Beach, I knelt and asked the Lord to preserve Astrea's life.

When I arrived at the apartment, the door to the bathroom had already been opened and upon entering I saw Astrea, slumped against the wall, clothes soaked in blood and with no apparent signs of life in her body.

I straddled her inert form, and crouching down, with my face close to hers, I demanded to know why the demon had returned. Astrea's eyelids flickered and she spoke in a voice that terrified the five members of the family who crowded the bathroom doorway. It announced that the chief of the legion of blood had come to take her to the grave.

It would be difficult to describe my emotions: blood was everywhere and I was face to face with a powerful demonic entity that intended to kill. I was simultaneously repulsed and terrified, but, almost before I was aware of it, a holy anger against this bloody demon swept over me and filled me with authority. In Jesus' name I demanded that the chief of the legion of blood return to the arid places of the world. The Lord Jesus Himself, I told him, was going to deliver Astrea out of his hands. A sound like that of a wounded animal welled up from her throat. After a terrible convulsion, Astrea fell over on the bathroom floor.

"She's dead," her husband gasped.

"No," I replied, "you are wrong. Astrea is truly alive for the first time in fifteen years."

A week or so later, I met Dr. Costas Rodrigues, the psychiatrist who had attended Astrea for years. She had been taken to a hospital to recover from this nightmare. The doctor assured me that, after some days of constant observation and a full physical examination, "whatever caused the attacks" had been completely healed.

Seven Crossroads

In January of 1973, a husband and wife who had been attending our services in the New Life Pentecostal Church in Rio de Janeiro came to ask for prayer. On the previous day, the woman had attacked her husband and beat him without mercy, in spite of the fact that he was a strong man weighing over two-hundred-fifty pounds. They lived in constant terror of attacks when a superhuman strength would come into her body and cause her to attack whoever was near.

Her name was Maria. When she was fifteen years old, she had joined a spiritist circle and given herself over to evil spirits. In the initiation ceremony, she killed a black hen by biting its neck and drinking its blood. For about fifteen years she had regularly given herself to this underworld force, called "exu."

After her marriage, Maria stopped attending these sessions, but was still bothered regularly by attacks during which she would have to be restrained and sometimes confined until the attack passed.

Maria and her husband attended our Sunday services for a number of months and began to wonder if God could deliver her from this demon spirit. I told her that following the Sunday evening meeting we would deal with the problem. I spent the afternoon in prayer to prepare for the encounter which, as it turned out, was the most violent in my twenty years of experience with evil spirits.

After most of the people had left the sanctuary, I called Dr. Tito Almeida, my associate, to accompany me. We began to talk with Maria and her husband. She told us that, in the churches where she had visited before, the demon had always manifested himself, but that he did not attack her when she was in our church. She informed us that *Sete Encruzilhadas* (Seven Crossroads, the name of the exu) would only possess her when he wanted and that he obeyed no one. And, she told us, she always knew when this demon was approaching and that he was not anywhere around.

However, when I called his name, the demon spirit literally threw Maria out of her chair, leaving her shoes where they were. Growling darkly, she began to foam at the mouth, crawling along the front of the church. I spoke to the demon in the name of Jesus and Maria's face turned to me. I have never seen a human face so twisted with hate. Her lips curled back and with bared teeth she rose up off the floor to attack me.

But she didn't reach me. I commanded the demon to go in the name of Jesus, and Maria's body was thrown to the floor. Then she rose again to attack me. It happened five or six times during this brief but terrible struggle. This blood-thirsty demon's rage was directed as much at Maria as at myself. Her body was thrown violently onto the floor without mercy. But I persisted in demanding that Seven Crossroads leave, never to return.

It happened in an instant. The attack was over as quickly as it had begun, leaving Maria bruised and exhausted.

"Pastor, is it over?"

"Maria, I believe the Holy Spirit wants me to tell you that this was the demon's final attack. You'll not be bothered again so long as you abide in Christ."

She and her husband began faithfully to attend the church services and at this writing are serving the Lord with gladness.

Twenty Years Of Trouble

These three cases of demonization are representative of the hundreds of such cases I have dealt with in the last score of years. In Europe, the Orient, and both North and South America, I have seen the loneliness, terror and helplessness caused by demons.

Following the Clarita incident, I ministered throughout the island of Taiwan. In almost every service people brought their relatives and friends to be delivered from demons. The demons would speak in Japanese and the pastors explained that since the Japanese occupation and because of the atrocities that accompanied it, the problem of demon possession had swollen so that public services were constantly interrupted by demonic manifestations.

In India I met the problem of evil spirits again. Preaching the gospel in a tent in downtown Calcutta, I was frequently interrupted by someone who was being attacked by demons. Each time it was necessary to confront the demonic power with the authority of the name of Jesus.

As I continued in the ministry of missionary evangelism my experience with the demon possessed broadened. In Paris a high percentage of those who came for healing were possessed by evil spirits, due to their previous contact with spiritism. Prayer for these people whose lives were dominated by demons was fruitless, and so I continued to learn the strength of our spiritual resources to exorcise demons through the power of Jesus' name.

I had begun to think that the problem of demonism only existed on foreign mission fields where paganism or spiritism were widely practiced. But, on my return to the United States, I found that demon activity was by no means so confined.

How well I remember the night that I cast a demon spirit from a young nurse who attended a service in the First Baptist Church in Burbank, California, where I was speaking. She had phoned me in response to a brief message I had preached on a local radio station. She had sold her soul to the devil in a witchcraft ceremony a number of years previously. Since then she had been confined, at various times, in three mental hospitals and was frequently subject to the terror of the demonic attacks. I urged her to come to the church that evening.

It was an experience that none of us who saw it will ever

forget. After the service, a large number of the church members were still gathered near the front of the church in casual conversation. When I confronted the demon that possessed the body of this slender, well-dressed woman, the air was rent by a piercing scream and her body was thrown to the carpeted floor of the sanctuary where she began to writhe like a snake.

Once again I drew on the authority of the powerful name of the Lord Jesus to bring freedom to this demonized woman. Once again light cast out darkness and she was liberated. Her letters tell me that she is free indeed, with no recurrence of the demonic attacks.

A Demon Of What?

During the years since 1951, on those occasions when I have been in the United States, I became aware of the gradual increase in demonic activity in our country, but I was still unprepared for a conversation with a young woman who leads a prayer group in a city on the East coast.

This rather plump, devoted child of God (let's call her Grace) told me with satisfaction that she had just been delivered from a demon of gluttony. In a sort of shock I asked her, "A demon of what?"

"Gluttony."

It seems that a friend of hers had recently been given a deliverance ministry and had cast the demon of gluttony out of Grace during a prayer meeting. I was dumfounded. I'd never heard of such a thing, but asked her to elaborate.

For many years Grace had fought a losing battle with her appetite. After a series of diets and exercises she had come to the conclusion that the problem was bigger than she was and that she just had to have help.

When she attended a prayer meeting with friends, the host told her that she had a demon of gluttony. Immediately Grace saw the reason for her inability to control her eating

23

and was overjoyed to know that there was a solution to her problem.

She sat in a chair in the middle of the room, while the others laid hands on her to pray for the exorcism of the demon. Grace told me that she went into a sort of trance and, in a vision, saw her mother who had died. She felt that this was a confirmation of the reality of her deliverance and, following a time of prayer and thanksgiving, left the meeting, rejoicing in her victory.

I was profoundly disturbed in spite of Grace's evident joy. She had walked into a trap by dealing with the problem of overeating in a way that would lastingly distort her entire experience of the Christian faith.

Since overeating is the antithesis of self-control, which is mentioned among the fruit of the Spirit in Galatians 5:22,23, gluttony should be classified with the carnal appetites described in Galatians 5:19-21 as the works of the flesh. And you do not cast out the flesh.

But how well do you tell this to a woman who has just had the "demon of gluttony" cast out of her? After years of undisciplined eating; of losing the battle of the flesh against the Spirit, her problem had been solved in an instant. But had it? What if the definition was wrong? What if there was no demon present to be exorcised? What if the brother who declared Grace to be demonized was wrong? I truly believe he was.

I remember a Chinese girl in the Philippine Islands who was dying of starvation because the demon that possessed her refused to allow her to eat. But I have never heard of a single case where a demon caused a person to overeat.

Eating and drinking provide strength for our physical bodies, but they can destroy us when done to excess. Any abuse of this normal physical appetite must be dealt with in a scriptural manner: through the walk in the Spirit whereby emerges the fruit of self-control.

I asked myself a very painful question: What would happen when Grace's appetite returned? Would she have to be delivered again? If she had a problem before the "deliverance" she surely would have a bigger one afterwards. For, added to her gluttony would be doubts and misgivings: Why did the demon return? Wasn't the prayer fervent enough? Was she unworthy of deliverance? Does God want to punish her in some way by allowing this demon of overeating to dominate her will?

I do not believe that you can cast out the flesh. But when you try, you are surely going to come into a place of confusion and condemnation.

The Demon Of Frivolity

A few weeks after my encounter with Grace, I was invited to a prayer group of dedicated believers, many of whom I knew personally. After giving a meditation on the Spirit-filled life, I opened the meeting for questions and was immediately asked whether or not I believed that Christians could be demon possessed.

I inquired, "Why do you ask such a thing?"

"A minister recently visited us and cast demons out of almost every one here."

I could hardly believe what I was hearing. This group had been told it was necessary to become aware of the presence of demons and to learn how to handle them. Demons, they were told, were the real sources of their longstanding personal problems.

"Has anyone of you ever seen a person who was really demon possessed?" I asked.

A silver-haired schoolteacher spoke up, "Just the other day I cast the demon of frivolity out of one of my pupils who would not pay attention in class." She beamed as she told me that he straightened right up. I guess he surely did. He was probably frightened out of his wits.

This had been my first contact with a renewal prayer group in almost a year. I began to find, as I traveled from city to city, an obsession with demons in almost every group that I visited. Their primary concern was in identifying and expelling demons from believers. I was utterly amazed.

The pastor of a large church in the Los Angeles area told me that the demons-in-believers doctrine had caused more trouble in his church than he would ever be able to repair. Another clergyman in Orange County, California, said that many believers would not get out of bed in the morning until they had cast out the demons that had entered during the night. Some parents were casting demons out of their grade school children before sending them off in the morning.

I discovered that, in those churches where there was a strong, Bible-centered ministry, the members had not been unsteadied by the doctrine of demonized believers. However, in most of the prayer groups that I contacted, there was considerable confusion about whether or not Christians could be possessed by evil spirits. Demons of sloth, nervousness, forgetfulness and all manner of carnal habits were being cast out.

So, why another book about demons? Because we need to seek an answer to the question of whether or not a true believer in the Lord Jesus Christ can be possessed by a demon. One pastor, when asked if a believer could have a demon, said, "Who wants one?" But I will not be satisfied with glib retorts. This is a serious matter and deserves a prayerful discussion of the questions that are being raised by born-again children of God, many of whom are deeply troubled over the question of demonism. May the Holy Spirit guide us into the truth.

Chapter II
DEMONS AND DEMON POSSESSION

Do Demons Really Exist,
Or Is This Just Superstition?

Jesus accepted the reality of demons. Many times, during His earthly ministry, He cast out demons. "And also some women who had been healed of evil spirits and sicknesses: Mary who was called Magdalene, from whom seven demons had gone out" (Luke 8:2).

The New Testament is filled with evidence to prove the existence of demons. Luke's Gospel tells about a man in the synagogue who was possessed by the spirit of an unclean demon (Luke 4:33). Mark describes in detail the malefic effects of demon possession in the case of the deaf and dumb boy, who, when demon possessed, was seized, dashed to the ground, foamed at the mouth, ground his teeth, and stiffened out. When Jesus cast out the unclean spirit, the boy was both healed and delivered (Mark 9:17-27). Matthew informs us about the ultimate destruction of demons. "Then He will also say to those on His left, 'Depart from Me, accursed ones, into the eternal fire which has been prepared for the devil and his angels' " (Matt. 25:41).

There can be no doubt from the testimony of Scripture, from the examples of history, as well as the multitudes of present-day occurrences, that demons are a reality.

What Are Demons, And Where Do They Come From?

It is impossible to be dogmatic about the origin of demons. Among the many theories, there is convincing Biblical evidence to support the one that says demons are fallen angels, that when Lucifer was cast down from heaven because of pride and rebellion (Isa. 14:12-15), he took with him a third of the heavenly host of angels (Rev. 12:4). These fallen angels are described in the Bible as demons or evil spirits. In His dialogue with the Pharisees in Matthew 12:24-28, Jesus talked about Satan and his demons.

How Many Kinds Of Demons Are There?

There is no way to know. Jesus asked one demon to identify himself and was told, "My name is Legion; for we are many" (Mark 5:9).

The Bible speaks of unclean spirits (Mark 3:11; 6:7), deaf and dumb spirits (Mark 9:25), evil spirits (Acts 19:12-13, 15-16), lying spirits (I Kings 22:22-23), a spirit of divination (Acts 16:16), the spirit of antichrist (I John 4:3), a spirit of infirmity (Luke 13:11) and others.

In primitive areas, demons will often identify themselves by names associated with local pagan worship. Sometimes they will call themselves by animal names, and the tormented demoniac will make the sounds and gestures appropriate of the name of the spirit that possesses him.

Satan, however, is the father of lies and his demons are

no better than their master. In order to disguise their presence, demons will tell all kinds of lies and call themselves by
almost any name. They will pretend to be almost anything
but what they really are. While it is possible to require a
demon to reveal his presence, it is useless to require him to
tell you his real identity. He will tell you anything you want
to hear, and most of it will be a lie.

What Is The Difference Between
The Devil And A Demon?

The Bible uses many names to describe the devil: Satan
(Matt. 12:26), Lucifer (Isa. 14:12 KJV), Beelzebub (Matt.
12:24). There is always a clear distinction made between this
singular person called the devil, and the host of demons.

Practictioners of spiritism in Brazil say the satanic trinity is composed of Satan, Lucifer, and the devil (in blasphemy
of the Holy Trinity). Each possesses different attributes and
carries out various functions. Demons are inferior, in no way
equal to the supreme authority of this supposed satanic
trinity.

Demons correspond to angels both in authority and
function. They always act in the name of their master and
carry out his will; but they do not have full satanic power, nor
do they perform the same function.

It is most important to understand the difference between Satan and his demons. People who live in contact with
someone who is demon possessed are often needlessly afraid
because they feel that Satan himself is present, when, in
reality, they have a much lesser enemy, a demon.

In his book, *Dealing with the Devil*, C.S. Lovett says, "I
want you to forget about demons. I am satisfied that their role
is minor." He is correct.

The most serious consequence of confusion between
satanism and demonism is that many attribute to demons

what is really the work of Satan, and thus they cast out demons that simply do not exist.

The Bible, in its original languages, clearly teaches the difference between the devil and a demon. The word "devil" comes from the Greek word *diabolos* which means "the slanderer." The word "Satan" comes from the Hebrew, *Satan* (see Job 2:1), and, when the Old Testament was rendered into Greek, the translators used the Greek *diabolos* to translate the Hebrew *Satan*. Though, by the time the New Testament was written, *Satan* had become a Greek word and is used in the New Testament beside *diabolos* (see Rev. 20:2). The words from which we derive our word "demon" are *daimonion* and *daimon*. There is never any confusion in the Scriptures between these distinct evil entities. Although this is not immediately clear in our English Bibles. For example, the King James, New English, Jerusalem and Phillips versions all translate *daimones* in Matthew 8:31 as "devils." The Revised Standard, Berkeley, New American Standard, Living, Amplified, and New International versions render it "demons," which is more accurate.

What Is The Difference Between Demon Possession And Satanic Oppression?

Serious problems result from confusion on this point. Simply stated, possession is demonic, while oppression is satanic. The former is an attack from the inside; the latter is an attack from the outside. Satan does not inhabit the human body. Jesus never cast Satan out of anyone, but He did cast demons out of those who were possessed.

In demon possession, the victim is dominated, body, soul, and spirit, by an evil spirit and is helpless to effect his own deliverance. I can find no Scriptural evidence to show that an obedient believer in Jesus can be possessed by a demon.

On the other hand, satanic oppression is a very real problem among God's children. We are told: "Resist the devil and he will flee from you" (James 4:7). We are never told to resist demons because they have no power over the life of a child of God.

What Are The Effects Of Satanic Oppression?

Satanic oppression results in a multitude of afflictions in the lives of both believers and nonbelievers.

Satanic oppression encourages the works of the flesh: "immorality, impurity, sensuality, idolatry, sorcery, enmities, strife, jealousy, outbursts of anger, disputes, dissensions, factions, envyings, drunkenness, carousings, and things like these" (Gal. 5:19-21). The devil schemes to bring believers into defeat. This is a part of the battle every Christian wages as his flesh wars against the Spirit.

The works of the flesh are not, as some suppose, a consequence of demon possession. Thus it is foolish to cast out a "spirit of anger" which is part of a person's nature, or a "spirit of stomach trouble" which results from wrong eating, or a nervous condition (unbelief) aggravated by satanic oppression.

You cannot cast out the flesh. It must be dealt with as sin which has to be confessed and cleansed by the blood of Christ. It would be delightful to take care of all fleshly desires, like anger and contention, by instant exorcism, but it just doesn't happen that way. People want it to happen that way, though, because they are unwilling to settle down to the hard business of living in Christ. There is no instant remedy for carnality. It is gradually cured by the walk in the Spirit.

Another consequence of satanic oppression is physical and emotional disease. Much illness, wrongly attributed to demons, is a result of oppression by the devil. "You know of

Jesus of Nazareth, how God anointed Him with the Holy Spirit and with power, and how He went about doing good, and healing all who were *oppressed by the devil*; for God was with Him" (Acts 10:38). Here are the ulcers, the skin diseases, the migraine headaches, and the endless list of infirmities that plague humanity. Does the Bible give us a solution to the problem of disease? "Is anyone among you sick? Let him call for the elders of the church, and let them pray over him, anointing him with oil in the name of the Lord; and the prayer offered in faith will restore the one who is sick, and the Lord will raise him up" (James 5:14-15). There is not one word here about demons or possession or exorcism.

The oppression of fleshly thoughts and actions, of emotional and physical sickness, are the work of Satan. It was Satan who went out from the presence of the Lord to smite Job with sickness (Job 2:7), not a demon spirit. Sickness is healed in the name of Jesus through His atoning work on Calvary (Isa. 53:5), not by the casting out of demons.

It must be added, however, that there are certain sicknesses that are caused by demon possession, and these will be discussed shortly.

Can A Person Be Satan Possessed?

The phrase, "He's full of the devil," is colloquial, not Biblical. The only instance where the Bible describes a person as Satan possessed is the case of Judas. "And Satan entered into Judas" (Luke 22:3). The forces of hell were marshaled against the Christ. No demonic agent was sufficient for this job. Satan himself entered into the traitor and carried out his evil work. However, this unique example does not give us margin to believe that anyone since that time has been inhabited by Satan.

32

What About The Daughter Of Abraham
Who Was Bound By Satan?
Wasn't She Satan Possessed?

In Luke 13:10-16, Jesus said that Satan had *bound* this daughter of Abraham for eighteen years. However, in the beginning of the narrative, Luke says that the woman had a sickness caused by a spirit. The King James version calls it a "spirit of infirmity."

Here a physical deformity (the woman was bent double, and couldn't straighten up) was caused by a demon. Notice carefully how Jesus delivered her. First He said, "Woman, you are *freed* from your sickness." In freeing her, Jesus broke the power of the demon and he left. In the following verse, Jesus laid His hands on her and she was healed. Jesus did not lay hands on the woman until He had first freed her from demonic power.

Some teachers use this story to show that believers can be demon possessed. This woman was a Jew, a daughter of Abraham. However, she was not—indeed she could not have been—a participant in the New Covenant. Jesus had not yet died and arisen nor had the Holy Spirit come to inhabit each believer.

If Demons Don't Oppress,
How Can Satan Alone Do So Much Damage?
Is He Omnipresent?

No. Satan does not possess any of the attributes of divinity. He is not omniscient, omnipresent or omnipotent, nor is he eternal.

Lucifer (by whatever Bible name we call him) is a created being; he was made in an angelic, not human, form. Had he been created in human form, he would suffer the limitations of time and space that restrict us all, and to which our Lord Himself submitted.

But Satan moves in the realm of the spirit, and here is where we begin to have real problems of definition. We do not understand what this dimension is, nor what its limitations are.

We must reject the delightful fiction of C.S. Lewis in *The Screwtape Letters* about Wormwood, the devil (demon) who had the job of destroying the faith of a believer. The idea of one devil per Christian is certainly not a Biblical concept, and we must enjoy Dr. Lewis' book for what it is: an absorbing description of the terrible problem of temptation and human frailty. As such it is much more beneficial to growth in Christ than books that depict exorcism as the pathway to maturity.

Because the Bible is clear that oppression is satanic, there is no way that we can make oppression demonic.

What Is Demon Possession?

To be possessed by a demon, or to be demonized, which is a more accurate translation of the Greek *daimonizomai*, is to be under control of an evil spirit. Every facet of the demoniac's personality is affected by the demon who inhabits and dominates him. His mind, speech, and actions are subject to the demon.

After a demon has been cast out of a person, he will often ask what he did while under the demon's influence. During his torment, a demoniac is not conscious of his actions or words.

Demonization can affect even one's physical appearance. I remember one time when a demon claimed to be an ancient Oriental. At this, the demon-possessed man took on an oriental facial expression. It was a terrifying experience for those who were present.

Frequently, changes occur in the voice. I have listened many times to a deep bass, male voice coming from the throat of a possessed woman. I have also heard demons speak in high-pitched, reedy tones, which were likewise quite different from those of the demoniac when he or she was not being tormented.

When a person is demon possessed, it is impossible to talk with him; all communication must be addressed to the demon who is in full control of both mind and voice.

Is A Demoniac Under Evil-Spirit Control Twenty-Four Hours A Day?

Very rarely have I found that a demon will remain in the same body day and night, even though he will claim each body he possesses as his "house." In Rio de Janeiro, I asked one demon spirit how long he had possessed the body of a certain woman, and I was told that he had been in that house for over ten years. Then he added, "Even though I live here, I go and torment many others." There were periods of time when this woman was not under the domination of the demon, and at those times she was rational and in control of all of her faculties.

The coming and going of demons is an important reason for the need of the Holy Spirit's gift of discerning of spirits. Many demons who have supposedly been cast out have merely left of their own accord in order to avoid a confrontation. When this happens there appears to be an easy victory, but, in reality, there isn't even battle. The demon simply returns to inhabit his house later, much to the consternation of all involved.

This is why I have found it so important to require a demon to reveal his presence. I habitually make him speak to me, so that I can be sure that he confesses his defeat and leaves the demoniac in peace.

Do Demons Really Talk?

They certainly do, and they are very articulate. Demons can be made to respond when they are challenged. I have spoken to demons on many occasions, and for periods of up to thirty minutes.

Jesus had dialogue with demons. "And the demons began to entreat Him, saying, 'If You are going to cast us out, send us into the herd of swine.' And He said to them, 'Begone' " (Matt. 8:31-32). Earlier in the same narrative, the demons had asked Jesus if He had come to torment them before their time.

When in possession of a human body, a demon will use his own voice, vocabulary and understanding. This is why a demoniac will not sound like himself; will say things far outside of his field of knowledge; will use a vocabulary unknown to him, and in some instances, even foreign languages. He is under the absolute control of the demon. The demoniac is merely an instrument to transmit the demon's voice.

Why Is It Necessary To Make A Demon Talk To You?

More than anything, a demon fears exposure. He will try desperately to distract observers from detecting his presence. Exposure leads to expulsion, and the demon knows that. Once he is unmasked, he will not stay and fight a losing battle against the power of the name of Jesus.

In Gadara, Jesus asked the demon to reveal his name, and was told, "My name is Legion; for we are many" (Mark 5:9). Do you suppose that Jesus didn't already know the name of the demon? Of course He did. Then why did He ask?

When a demon is required to speak, even though he will probably respond to questioning with lies, he is no longer hidden. I remember one woman who was brought to me for help, against her will. For many months she had manifested symptoms of demon possession, but attended our church services for a full month without any torment. The evil spirit would not show himself, although he must have been very uncomfortable during those services of praise to God. Finally the day came when I challenged the demon to speak to me. This exposure led to the woman's immediate deliverance.

Why Do Demons Have To Possess A Human Body?

Demons must have a body through which to manifest themselves. The Bible describes the problem this way: "When the unclean spirit goes out of a man, it passes through waterless places seeking rest, and not finding any, it says, 'I will return to my house from which I came' " (Luke 11:24).

It is evident that a demon finds satisfaction and rest in having a body as his house, his place of activity. And demons become very possessive and jealous of the bodies they inhabit.

During a communion service in a Brazilian church, a demon began to manifest himself in loud and vile language. When I challenged him in the name of Jesus, he was indignant that I would dare to cast him out and told me, "This has been my house for nineteen years."

A human body gives a demon great latitude of activity. Because humans have the power of speech, their bodies are preferable to those of animals. There are times, however, when even animals become the "houses" of demons (Mark 5:12).

How Does A Person Become Demon Possessed?

The Bible tells us how a person who has once been delivered from demons could become repossessed (Luke

11:24-26), but it does not tell us specifically how a person initially becomes demonized.

I have questioned hundreds of demoniacs in detail after their deliverance to find the answer to this important question, and I have learned that the following kinds of people are easy prey to demons:

1) Those who lead immoral lives.

2) Those who live in voluntary, persistent sin.

3) Those who involve themselves in the occult practices to receive answers to questions or solutions to their problems.

4) Those who use hallucinatory drugs.

5) Those who become hypnotized for the purpose of divination, fortune telling, or levitation.

6) Those who expose their minds to psychic phenomena or practice the passive meditations of the Eastern religions.

7) Those who willfully misrepresent God, as in the case of a young woman I knew who controlled a church through false prophecy. She had started doing it as a joke, but in the end, she was completely demon possessed.

8) Anyone who is not born again of the Spirit of God may become demonized.

The only sure protection against possession by evil spirits is the blood of Jesus Christ, the forgiveness of sins, and a life of obedience and faith.

What Are The Symptoms Of Demon Possession?

An abnormal voice and distorted facial expression almost inevitably occur. Violence and demon possession are inseparable, and demoniacs are usually abnormally aggressive. Many times a jealous demon will cause his victim to try to destroy the person closest to him. One demon-possessed woman tried to set fire to the bed while her husband slept. In most cases, violence is directed toward anyone who happens to be near.

Self-inflicted violence is common. One woman was brought to me whose body was covered with hundreds of small knife wounds inflicted over a period of two years. Often self-destruction will take the form of inability to swallow food. I have already mentioned the case of the daughter of a prominent Chinese businessman in Manila, whose weight had dropped to less than fifty pounds, and no amount of persuasion could make her take food or drink. After a demon was cast out, she sat down within the hour to a delicious meal.

Superhuman strength is another mark of the demon possessed. I have seen frail women terrorize entire families while possessed. In one instance, four strong ushers were needed to restrain a sixteen-year-old girl who suffered a demon attack as she began to enter the door of our church. Evidently the evil spirit who possessed her had no intention of becoming involved in a gospel service.

Unusual knowledge and clever reasoning are often present in a demoniac. This explains the phenomena of spirit-writing, telepathy, and many related psychic phenomena. Some demoniacs speak with the knowledge of people of other lands and cultures. In Brazil, one famous medium speaks with the vocabulary of a German doctor who, he claims, lived in the eighteenth century. This, and other cases like it, have been cited in favor of the doctrine of reincarnation. But the voices are those of demons who impersonate people long dead. This kind of thing fascinates people and by it many have become victims of demonic influence and often of actual demon possession.

An unusual incident along this line happened to me one time when I was preaching in a church in Cumberland, Maryland. A woman stood and interrupted me to inform the members of the church that a minister who was known to them was passing through Mau-Mau territory in East Africa on that night, and that he (the evil spirit) planned to kill that minister and his companions.

Although this could have been an authentic gift of knowledge from the Holy Spirit, her manner alarmed me. By discernment I perceived that she was speaking by demonic inspiration, and, after casting the demon out of the woman, I suggested that the entire congregation pray for the protection of that minister and his party. We later verified that, on the night in question, he and three others were traveling in Kenya, through the heart of the bloody Mau-Mau uprising.

Another possible symptom of possession is religiosity. Demons may try to mask their presence with religious talk. They will speak flatteringly of Jesus and sound very spiritual. These lying spirits can easily deceive those who do not discern their presence by the power of the Holy Spirit.

Sometimes demoniacs will be struck dumb and will only respond when commanded to do so in the name of Jesus. Others may suffer from lockjaw, while others will simply shake their heads and remain mute until obliged by the authority of Christ to reply. In each of these cases the demon hopes to remain hidden behind his victim's silence.

Can You Always Tell By These Symptoms Whether Or Not A Person Is Demon Possessed?

No one symptom or combination of symptoms prove that a person is demon possessed. Many people are violent, use foul and blasphemous language, but they are not possessed by a demon.

Nor are nervous disorders, such as twitching, profuse perspiring, or extreme agitation, proof of demon possession, although they sometimes indicate the presence of a demon.

Symptoms must never determine a diagnosis of demonization. We must always be finally dependent on the guidance of the Holy Spirit. Otherwise we will be in danger of really hurting someone by trying to exorcise them on the flimsy evidence of uncertain symptoms.

Can More Than One Demon Possess The Same Body?

Yes, in fact, it is so, more often than not. In the case of the woman possessed by demons from the "legion of blood," I identified two demons, and, on the fifth and final encounter, a third demon said that he was the chief of the legion of blood.

In the narrative in Mark 5:9, the demon described himself as Legion, an indication that there were many.

How Can You Tell If More Than One Demon Possesses A Demoniac?

Most of the time by asking questions. It is possible to confront a demon very plainly, requiring of him (or them, in the case of multiple possession) a reply to your questions. Remembering that demons are expert liars whose purpose is to confuse, you can never be certain that the names they give are accurate, but you can determine whether or not there are more than one present.

Demonic activity declines as the evil spirits leave the body. Final deliverance is assured when the victim confesses Jesus Christ as his Lord and Savior. No one who has ever dealt with demon possession is in any doubt when the battle is over and every spirit cast out.

Do All Demons Have The Same Power?

The longer a demon possesses a body, the stronger will be his power over that person. When the possession has continued for many years, the demon will violently resist any

41

attempt to cast him out. This, however, is not invariably the case. Some demons will obey the word of authority in Jesus' name without much of a struggle, while others resist until the battle becomes titanic.

Are Demons Ever Related To A Specific Place, Such As A Haunted House?

This is an interesting question. From the many cases of demon possession I have encountered, certain patterns begin to emerge. One is the very positive connection between the manifestation of evil spirits and certain rooms, or houses, or buildings. In Rio de Janeiro I dealt with a woman who became demon possessed when she went into a certain room of her house. When she left, she was perfectly free of torment.

I have visited places, both indoors and out, where pagan and spiritistic ceremonies were performed, and was aware, through the Holy Spirit, that I was in a residence of demons. But I suffered no ill effects from being in those places since I was under Christ's protection.

When demons are cast out, they remain only in places conducive to their activities. For example, when a demoniac is brought to a church and set free, the demon will not remain in the church to attack others. The hostile environment affords him no rest. The Bible describes the habitat of demons as among ruins in desolate places that have felt the stroke of God's judgment (Lev. 16:10; Isa. 13:19-22; 34:13-14). The "waterless places" mentioned in Matthew 12:43 where demons roam after expulsion are undoubtedly the heavenly places Paul mentions in Ephesians 6:12 by which he meant the atmosphere surrounding the earth. This helps us understand Satan's title as the prince of the power of the air (Eph. 2:2).

Where Do Demons Feel At Home?

Demons can enter a human body only when that person has created conditions conducive to possession through willful and persistent sin, or where they have been exposed to demonic power through occult practices or the like and do not have the protection of the cleansing blood of Christ. A demon can remain in a body only as long as those conditions remain constant.

I have known scores of people who have come to our church services, accepted the Lord Jesus as Savior, been baptized in water, and later filled with the Holy Spirit. They have described their former lives so that it seemed beyond a shadow of doubt that they were truly demon possessed prior to their salvation. But there was no exorcism.* At the moment of salvation, the conditions that permitted the possession were radically changed. On returning to his "house," the demon found it occupied by Jesus.

Those who teach that there is a "demonic residue" in those who had dabbled in the occult, even after their conversion, simply do not understand the nature of full salvation. He whom the Son sets free is free indeed, and this includes freedom from any previous contact with demons. This, of course, by no means precludes the necessity for new converts—even Christians of long standing—to confess and receive absolution for occult practices before or after baptism.

---

*Interestingly, the Roman Catholic rite of baptism includes an act of exorcism.

Must We Keep Our Eyes Closed When Someone Is Casting Out Demons?

I remember a night in 1947 when a minister was conducting a mass-healing service in a stadium in Vancouver, Canada. At one point in the service he told the audience of over ten thousand people that he was going to cast out an evil spirit and that, if anyone looked up, he would probably be possessed instantly by the evil spirit who would immediately be looking for another victim. I can still feel the fear that entered that stadium as thousands of believers squeezed their eyes tightly shut hoping that demon wouldn't get into them.

Both the evangelist's warning and the fear he provoked in the people were the result of ignorance. Even if we don't know much about demonic forces, surely we should know that the power of Jesus to protect us from evil is greater than that.

What this evangelist did was completely unnecessary, but it's by many similar teachings among God's people today that unnecessary fear and much confusion is being brought into the Body of Christ. I pray that the Lord will give us understanding concerning His power.

Can A Person Who Lives In A House With A Demoniac Become Possessed?

Demon possession is not hereditary, nor is it a contagious disease that can be caught from a relative or friend. A child might, in consequence of his parents being demon possessed, live in the environment that permitted demons to act in the first place. Should the child, or anyone who lives in the same house, also lead a sinful life, he, too, is in danger of demon possession.

One of our young women in Brazil became demon possessed. No one could understand how such a thing could happen to this babe in Christ. Later, however, we learned that her profession of faith had not been genuine. This new convert had listened to the seductive lies of Satan and entered into a conspiracy of deceit in relation to a large amount of money she won on a television program. Having turned her back on the Lord, she had exposed herself to the enemy and became an easy prey to his attacks.

But that in itself was not sufficient to produce demonization. The catalyst was the girl's mother, a spiritistic medium who practiced the black art of witchcraft daily. She came to live with her daughter just about the same time the girl had withdrawn herself from divine protection by yielding to satanic temptation. She was Satan's mouthpiece in the girl's ear, urging her to believe she had done nothing wrong. Only after she sent her mother back home was it possible for the daughter to get deliverance. Today this young woman is back in the church, happily serving the Lord and aware of her need to walk with God in honesty and obedience.

Do Some Demon-Possessed People Want To Stay That Way?

I knew a woman who tried three times to kill her husband. She was possessed by an unclean spirit with whom she achieved sexual satisfaction so that she locked herself in her room for days at a time. When the husband brought her to me for deliverance, she was not interested. She no longer loved her husband and didn't want to discuss her problem. When the demon manifested himself, we heard the whole perverse story.

But this woman's unwillingness to cooperate did not prevent us from casting out the unclean spirit and then, when the woman was not under his influence, explaining the Gospel of salvation to her. She was wonderfully saved from her sin, and her demonic boyfriend was unable to re-enter.

Generally, demonized people will not ask for help or deliverance. We might conclude from this that demon-possessed people want to stay that way, but this is not so. Many demoniacs realize that they need help, and some even come voluntarily to seek deliverance. Most often, though, relatives or close friends bring them for exorcism since the demon has an iron grip on their wills.

Has There Ever Been A Case Where The Victim Collaborated With The Demon And Deliverance Was Impossible?

I know of only one instance. It happened in Rio de Janeiro and involved a young man named Gilberto to whom we had ministered during a period of seven years. When Gil first came to our services, his demonization was dealt with, and he was wonderfully delivered. He gave us to understand that he was very happy and relieved.

We didn't see Gil for about two years. When he returned, he was again possessed by the unclean spirit. Once again we used the authority of the name of Jesus and cast out the spirit. Once again, Gil thanked us and disappeared.

Five years later he came back with the facial expression of one who is totally possessed by demons. I left him alone for almost a full month, and then, after one week-night service, I called the pastors and elders of the church, and we told Gil to stay after the service.

Once again we identified the demon as an unclean spirit, and for three hours we struggled against his demonic power. Finally the demon spoke and said, "It's just no use. You cast me out twice before and Gil came back and looked for me. He is corrupt and immoral, just as I am, and it's a perfect marriage. He has no interest in being saved and only wants to live the kind of immoral life that I can help him to live."

I commanded the evil spirit in Jesus' name to leave so that I could speak directly to Gilberto. He confessed to all of us that, following each of his previous exorcisms, he had returned to the low-spiritism group where he had been possessed as a boy. He said that he had no interest in salvation from his sins, and just wanted to be left alone to live his own life. When I asked him why he returned to the church, he replied that it was just out of curiosity to see what we would try to do for him. It was with great sadness that we watched Gil leave the church.

Thousands of people to whom I have preached the Gospel over the years have rejected God's offer of salvation, preferring to live in their sin. And, when Gilberto's rejection of mercy was connected with demon possession, it made his refusal of salvation all the more terrible.

Gil was in touch with the Gospel from time to time over this seven-year period, and at no time did he make a full surrender to Christ as his Lord and Savior. His return to demonism was voluntary and made it impossible for us to block the demon's return.

What Is The Ultimate Fate Of Demons?

The Bible teaches the ultimate punishment of Satan: "And the devil . . . was thrown into the lake of fire and brimstone, where the beast and the false prophet are also; and they will be tormented day and night forever and ever" (Rev. 20:10).

The punishment of demons is similarly described: "Depart from Me, accursed ones, into the eternal fire which has been prepared for the devil and his angels" (Matt. 25:41).

Demons, those fallen angels who were expelled from heaven with Lucifer, and who have done his bidding during the generations of human history, will be destroyed, together with their master in eternal flames.

Chapter III
DEMONS AND SICKNESS

Is All Sickness Caused By Demons?

There is a direct connection between demon possession and some types of sickness. I have never known a demoniac who was completely well in his body. But to attribute every sort of illness to evil spirits is pure fantasy.

We recognize many other causes for sickness: birth defects and accidents, exposure to communicable disease, the improper care of the body through overeating, inadequate rest, poor nutrition, etc. Certainly none of these things can be attributed to demons.

Those of us who have had major illnesses have grappled with the many-faceted problem of pain and sickness. While sickness is obviously destructive, it can also be a school for learning about God and ourselves in a profound dimension. Many of us who, through overwork and "burning out for God" (to use a familiar evangelical phrase), have been laid aside by illness, have learned that sickness can be redemptive, saving us from an untimely death.

There are many diseases, however, that cannot be attributed to such causes. What is their origin? Medical science says that many diseases are caused by mental and emotional disturbances. Some go so far as to attribute 85% of all sickness to these non-organic causes. One group of medical researchers affirms that without emotional tension, no disease can fasten itself on the human organism. In his excellent book, *None of These Diseases*, Dr. S.I. McMillen gives startling evidence of the destructive effects of fear on the body, the debilitating consequences of wrong thinking, and the intimate relationship between sickness and sin. In, *Release from Tension*, Dr. Paul E. Adolph shows how an unforgiving spirit, feelings of anger and jealousy, unthankfulness and pride, result in physical illnesses of all kinds.

What, or who, is the cause of all of this sickness-producing fear, tension, and carnal thinking? The answer is to be found in the Bible: It is Satan who robs us of our peace in God, who steals our joy, and who plagues us with all manner of sickness and disease. In I Peter 5:8 we read that our adversary is the devil. He is the source of fear, and the one who inspires anger and jealousy. It is Satan who attacks the mind and the nervous system, bringing about all sorts of depression and related physical illness.

Peter knew the truth of this matter when he told the household of Cornelius, "You know of Jesus of Nazareth, how God anointed Him with the Holy Spirit and with power, and how He went about doing good, and healing all who were *oppressed by the devil*; for God was with Him" (Acts 10:38, italics mine).

Satan can be resisted and his works destroyed. "Resist the devil and he will flee from you" (James 4:7). There is a cure for sickness. "And the prayer offered in faith will restore the one who is sick, and the Lord will raise him up" (James 5:15).

In the face of this evidence, it is surprising how many Christians attribute every ache and pain to the work of demons. And so, instead of using the prayer of faith, they look for someone who has the "ministry of deliverance" who will cast a demon out of them. Almost all sickness is the result of a satanic attack and can be dealt with simply and effectively by faith and prayer in the name of the Lord Jesus.

Can There Be A Demon Affliction Of The Mind And Not Of The Body?

Satan himself has free access to our minds and does most of his harvesting in them. All temptation to sin begins in the mind. This kind of oppression is one of his master tools to bring Christians into defeat.

Demons possess the bodies of their victims in order to subdue and control the thinking process as well as all other bodily functions. A demoniac is mentally disturbed, but this is a consequence of possession. The soul, which is the area of reason and emotion, is controlled completely by the evil spirit, while the body becomes a vehicle of demonic expression. It is only in this sense that his mind is affected.

This question grows out of a misunderstanding of what demon possession really does to a person. Some people teach that a person's mind can be possessed by demons, but not his body; or that the body can be possessed by demons, but not the soul. This theory does not agree with anything that I have learned, either by experience or Bible study.

The real problem of such unscriptural definitions is the confusion they bring to the people of God who are constantly involved in the real warfare of the flesh against the Spirit. Let us know our adversary so we can defeat him.

Are The Symptoms Of Oppression And Possession The Same Except In The Matter Of Intensity?

No. The difference between satanic oppression and demonic possession lies in the source. Satan oppresses, while demons possess.

God gives us the power to defeat all of Satan's attacks, be they of a spiritual, emotional, or physical nature. Our weapons are truth, righteousness, peace, faith, salvation, the Word of God, and prayer (Eph. 6:13-18).

There is another marked distinction between oppression and possession. Demons possess the unsaved, while Satan primarily attacks the children of God. There is no way for demons to possess a believer who is cleansed by the blood and sealed unto the day of redemption, and there is little reason for Satan to attack an unsaved man who is already his. That is the reason why many people, who do not believe, lead relatively unmolested lives. How many of your unsaved friends seem to breeze through life without the intense struggles that you face as a Christian?

You, not the unbeliever, are Satan's enemy. He will attempt to destroy your peace through impure thoughts; to kill your desire for spiritual things through the strong attraction of carnal pleasure; and to destroy your confidence in God by bringing emotional conflict that leads to sickness and disease. At a more subtle level, he tries to lull us into spiritual lethargy by telling us what we want to hear, that we are fine Christians who have reached an advanced state of maturity and can therefore relax.

When A Person Attempts Suicide, Is That A Proof That He Is Demon Possessed?

Almost without exception, a demoniac will sooner or later make an attempt on his own life. Many of those who had been delivered from demon possession told me that, if they had not actually attempted suicide, they thought about it constantly as a means of escape from the torment to which they were subject.

Most suicides, however, are the result of satanic oppression rather than demon possession. A demon must have a live body through which to operate. In those cases where suicide occurs in relation to demon possession, it is the demoniac who ends his own life in order to be free from the demon, and not the demon who kills his victim, for this would leave the demon without a body through which to act and talk.

Satan attacks the minds of men. He blinds them (II Cor. 4:4), hardens them (II Cor. 3:14), corrupts the minds of believers through false teaching (II Cor. 11:3), and makes depraved the minds of those who oppose the truth (II Tim. 3:8).

Satan does not need a human body through which to move and talk, and has no compunction about destroying a human life. Suicide, which is the ultimate rejection of life and obviates further repentance, is the tool of Satan, whose declared purpose is to kill and destroy (John 10:10).

Can Deafness Be Caused By Demons?

There are a number of sicknesses that may be caused by demons, and deafness is one of them. In the narrative of the epileptic boy (Mark 9:17-27), we find that he was afflicted by an unclean spirit with at least three sicknesses: deafness, dumbness, and convulsions.

I have already mentioned that many times the deafness and dumbness of a demoniac is merely the way in which the demon masks his presence. When it is ascertained through the gift of discerning spirits that the malady was caused by a demon, it is possible to require the demon to speak. Healing is effected when he is cast out.

But deafness is not always the result of demon possession. It can be caused by a perforated eardrum. And here is where great harm can be done by those who cast out a demon as a matter of routine whenever someone who is deaf is brought to them for healing. When you cast the "demon of deafness" out of someone who has a perforated eardrum you have given a wrong definition of the problem, often with tragic consequences.

First, you have wrongly accused someone who is possibly a child of God of being demon possessed. You have thus condemned that person to seek deliverance from something that is not present, and created a situation that will bring him into condemnation and spiritual defeat. Why didn't the Lord hear the prayer? Why didn't the demon go? Why doesn't deliverance work?

Much that is called a "deliverance ministry" is causing havoc in the lives of the spiritually immature and the emotionally unstable. Surely it is time to review this whole subject in the light of common sense and ask the Holy Spirit of God to show us just how we are to find real deliverance from both satanic oppression and physical sickness.

Is Fear Caused By Demon Possession?

The King James version of II Timothy 1:7 uses the phrase, "the spirit of fear," although other translations call it "a spirit of timidity," "a spirit of cowardice," or "a spirit that shrinks from danger." The question remains: Is fear an evil spirit?

The problem of fear is very complex. It can be caused by any number of natural circumstances, such as the lack of money to pay bills, or living in a dangerous neighborhood. There are other kinds of fears which we call complexes. They run the gamut from the fear that people don't like us to the fear that we are inadequate for our job. Other fears are more serious in their consequences, such as the obsession that we will become sick or have an accident. These fears often produce real sickness.

Beyond these kinds of fear, there is an unreasonable, destructive, and paralyzing fear that can be attributed only to Satan. I have dealt with many victims of this oppressive fear who were not, however, demon possessed. In these cases, the prayer of faith in Jesus' name was sufficient to bring about healing.

It is in borderline cases, where the symptoms indicate the possibility of demon possession, but where in reality they are caused by satanic oppression, that great and often permanent damage is done when a nonexistent demon is cast out.

Anyone who suffers from fear in this dimension, once he is told that he is demon possessed, is unable to handle the untrue accusation, and may be pushed beyond hope. Great wisdom and discernment must be used in order not to throw this person into crushing despair, and even suicide.

Finally, it must be stated that fear and terror are an automatic consequence in every case of demon possession, even in those rare cases when the victim cooperates with the demon. There is no question that one of the manifestations of an evil spirit is to submerge the personality of a demoniac in abject terror and utter despair.

Is Epilepsy The Same As Demon Possession?

This is a difficult question, since there is so much that is still unknown about the nature of this sickness. The editors of the New American Standard Bible chose to use the word "epileptic" in their paragraph heading to the narrative of the demon-possessed boy who was thrown into the fire with convulsions (Matt. 17:15-18). I don't know why they came to this conclusion, except that convulsions are also a manifestation of epilepsy. The father described his son as being a lunatic, not an epileptic.

In 1962, in the city of Niteroi, Brazil, I prayed for a six-year-old girl whose condition was diagnosed as epilepsy. She had fallen into convulsions without warning (grand mal) since birth. Her mother came to one of our evangelistic meetings and asked for prayer. We agreed together for the healing of little Rosane with no thought of exorcism. When the mother returned home, she found her daughter completely healed. Today both she and her mother are faithfully serving the Lord. In another case a mother brought her epileptic twelve-year-old boy to our meetings in Paris. Five weeks later, on the final day of the campaign, that youngster gave testimony to his complete healing from epilepsy.

Many people equate epilepsy with demon possession, because of the convulsions, foaming at the mouth, and the loss of memory which are common to both problems. However, epilepsy will respond to the prayer of faith for healing. In the two cases mentioned here, I did not discern the presence of an evil spirit. I do not eliminate the possibility, however, of having to cast out an evil spirit from someone whose condition has been diagnosed as epileptic. When, through the discerning of spirits, I recognize the presence of a demon, then I put aside all previous diagnoses, and deal directly with the demonic entity. But to say that all epilepsy is due to demon possession would surely be a mistake.

Is Drunkenness
A Symptom Of Demon Possession?

I have heard of a number of instances recently where "demons of drunkenness" have been cast out of people. I wonder if somebody got the idea from Billy Sunday's sermon, "Demon Rum."

Drunkenness is one of the works of the flesh (Gal. 5:21).

It is just one of the many things that an unsaved man will give himself to, including acts of immorality and idolatry, fits of anger and jealousy, etc.

As desirable as "instant sanctification" might be, these sins cannot be cast out, but must be dealt with through confession and the forgiveness of sin. The cure for drunkenness is salvation through the blood of the Lord Jesus Christ, the putting off of the body of the sins of the flesh in the waters of baptism (Col. 2:11-12), and the infilling of the Holy Spirit.

How Can You Tell Whether Or Not An Illness Is Caused By A Demon?

When sickness is the result of demon possession, there will be other symptoms such as violence, blasphemy, convulsions, etc. A very small percentage of sicknesses are caused directly by demon possession.

When a demon is expelled from one who is sick, the sickness disappears automatically at the time of deliverance. A young mother who had suffered with numerous afflictions for years was brought to my office for healing. When I laid my hands on her, the Holy Spirit revealed to me the presence of evil spirits. I removed my hands from her head and commanded the demons to leave her body. She fell to the floor, foaming at the mouth, and the evil spirit identified himself as *Sete Cabecas* (seven heads), one of the most powerful and feared demons of the low-spiritism practiced in Brazil. This woman was set free from the power of the demon and healed instantly of the sicknesses that had plagued her for years. She is a member of our church in Rio de Janeiro, well in body and sound of mind.

When sickness is caused by a demon, it is a consequence of demonization and not of attack from without. The phrase, "demonic attack," in relation to sickness, is just as unscriptural as the phrase, "satanic possession." A demon attack will only occur when there is demon possession. This is why it is foolish to cast out "evil spirits of headache," or "demons of stomach trouble." Surely Satan must laugh at the parlor games of those who attempt to heal the sick by casting out demons.

Chapter IV
BELIEVERS AND DEMON POSSESSION

Can A True Believer Be Possessed By A Demon?

We must make a clear distinction between true believers and church members who are not true believers. Not everyone whose name appears on the church roll is a sincere believer. I have known many churchgoers who discovered the life of Christ only after many years.

A man came to a retreat in the mountains of North Carolina where I was ministering. He told me that, after spending his entire lifetime in an evangelical church, he had received Jesus Christ as Lord and Savior just two months before the retreat.

In Rio de Janeiro, an Episcopalian woman, who had sung morning prayers every Sunday for over forty years in the English speaking church, came to our Wednesday night service where, according to her own testimony, she heard the Gospel of salvation for the first time in her life. Of course, she had, in one sense, heard it all her life, but, that night, she was wonderfully born again by the Spirit of God and found eternal life. Had you asked her if she were a Christian prior to that, she would have pointed to her membership in Christ Church and her service in the choir and women's society as irrefutable credentials. Afterward, however, she recognized that she had not had a personal experience with Christ Himself.

Let us, then, define a true believer. He is one who has been graced by God to seek forgiveness of his sin through Jesus according to Ephesians 1:7. The Holy Spirit resides in him and he walks in newness of life after being baptised in water (Rom. 6:4). He produces the fruit of the Spirit (Gal. 5:22-23). Jesus said, "You will know them by their fruits." When a true believer consistently trusts and obeys the Lord, it is impossible for him to become demon possessed.

A true believer is the purchased possession of God. "Or do you not know that your body is a temple of the Holy Spirit who is in you, whom you have from God, and that you are not your own? For you have been bought with a price; therefore glorify God in your body" (I Cor. 6:19-20). This temple of the Holy Spirit has received a seal of protection that will last until the day of our complete redemption. "And do not grieve the Holy Spirit of God, by whom you were sealed for the day of redemption" (Eph. 4:30). In spite of this and the further Biblical assertion that light has no fellowship with darkness, there are still those who would subject us to fears of demonic powers.

Books that defend the demons-in-believers theory make statements like this: "Theoretically it is not possible for a believer to be demon possessed, but experience seems to prove otherwise." I disagree. When there is a conflict between the Word of God and personal experience, it means we have misinterpreted the experience. You might also read about "certain uncommitted areas of your life" that can be possessed by evil spirits. But that is nonsense. Those uncommitted areas are pockets of darkness that must be confessed and renounced. Satan loves them and plays on them, but those who would attribute them to demons are only looking for ways to avoid the humiliation of confession and the taking up of the cross.

Can A Believer Who Turns His Back On God And Lives In Willful Sin Become Demon Possessed?

A woman was brought to my study after she tried to kill her two sons. She had been born and raised in a Christian home, but was evidently unconverted herself. She had suffered from, so it was thought, epileptic attacks throughout her youth and adulthood. I discerned demons and cast them out of her in Jesus' name. Later I learned that this woman had begun to prophesy in the church when she was just nine years old. She had made a game of interrupting the preacher while she gave her sanctimonious "prophetic utterance." One day she recognized that it was no longer she who was speaking, but another spirit that was in her. From that day forward she was demon possessed, and actually misled an evangelical church for a number of years through demon-inspired prophecies.

Her willful sin, the blasphemous imitation of a spiritual gift, led to demon possession.

Another young woman, also born and raised in a Christian home, was brought to me for deliverance from demons. And she *was* demon possessed. Her good looks had gotten her into television and theatrical work where she in turn practiced gross immorality. Demonization had resulted.

Neither of these women were clearly true believers prior to their demonization. Both of them had, however, some pretty serious exposure to the Gospel in their childhoods, and we cannot be sure that they hadn't had some genuine experience of new birth in those years. I think they may have, and I conclude from their experiences that the answer to our question is yes.

The promises of God's protection are all conditional. "If we walk in the light as He Himself is in the light . . . the blood of Jesus His Son cleanses us from all sin" (I John 1:7). When we fail to walk in the light, we remove ourselves from both fellowship and protection. This is why Paul tells us that we must not go on presenting the members of our body to sin as instruments of unrighteousness (Rom. 6:13).

Does This Mean That If We Misuse Spiritual Gifts We Are In Danger Of Becoming Demon Possessed?

The woman I just mentioned, who became demon possessed through false prophecy, did not do this in ignorance. It was calculated and stubborn blasphemy whereby she insisted that what she was saying off the top of her head was from God. There is no danger that someone would become demon possessed through the ignorant misuse of the gifts of the Holy Spirit. Our Heavenly Father would certainly not punish our immaturity by allowing demons to possess us.

Do Demons Have The Liberty To Repossess A Person Who Has Been Born Again?

When one receives Jesus as his Lord and Savior, Jesus frees him from the power of his sinful nature and from the bondage of demons, if there be any. "Therefore if any man is in Christ, he is a new creature; the old things passed away; behold, new things have come" (II Cor. 5:17).

A true understanding of salvation will answer all questions about the effects of a sinful past. "Therefore he is able to save completely those who come to God through him, because he always lives to intercede for them" (Heb. 7:25 NIV). This salvation avails for the sins of the past, and bestows upon us a totally new nature with which we begin to serve God.

Those who teach that there is a demonic residue in any believer because of contact with occult religions prior to salvation do not understand the nature of our redemption. (See question one in this part, Can a True Believer Be Possessed by a Demon?)

What Happens When Someone Attempts To Cast Demons Out Of A True Believer?

I was told about a young man in California who had been saved from a life of immorality, drug experiences, and involvement with the occult. He had walked with the Lord faithfully for five years, and during the last two of those years had obeyed God by helping other young people whose lives were warped by drugs and occult experiences. During that time, this young man's pastor came to believe that demons could inhabit believers. So, in spite of the young man's fruitful life, his pastor began to cast various demons out of him.

The man who told me this story had led this young fellow to Christ five years previously. With strong emotion, he told me how, for the past five months, this fine Christian worker had been confined in a psychiatric hospital as a result of a "deliverance session" with a man who reasoned that there must be a demonic residue from past experiences with drugs and the occult.

It would be possible to document scores of cases like this. Many pastors have told me about parishioners of theirs who have gone to prayer meetings where demons were supposedly spit up, only to return to their home church obsessed by the topic of demons. A woman came to me in tears after I once preached on this subject. She said I had saved her life.

A terror of demons had plagued her since the night she went with Christian friends to a "deliverance session." She was so relieved to know that, as a child of God, she was safe from evil spirits.

In What Way Can A Christian Be "Attacked By Demons"?

In no way whatever. Demons do not attack; they possess the bodies of people whose lives have invited their entrance. Here I need only briefly reiterate the basic distinction between the work of Satan and that of his demons. They are allied, but they have different methods. What Christians experience, and what they must learn to deal with, are the attacks of Satan.

It is wrong to think that demons are all around you, just waiting for some lapse of holiness so that they can jump on you or enter your body. Yet, typically, one "deliverance minister" has written: "The fact that one is a Christian does not assure that every area of his life is free from demonic bondage." I have followed in the wake of his ministry and find fear and confusion. Terrible things are being done in the name of deliverance. I pray God will deliver us from these deliverers.

Isn't It True That In The Last Days Many Christians Will Become Demon Possessed By Giving Heed To Seducing Spirits?

This question refers to Paul's warning to Timothy: "But the Spirit explicitly says that in later times some will fall away from the faith, paying attention to deceitful spirits and doctrines of demons" (I Tim. 4:1). Notice that, first, they will fall away from the faith. After that, they will begin to pay attention to deceitful spirits and doctrines of demons. In order to become deceived and pay heed to the doctrine of demons, it is first necessary to leave sound doctrine and wander in the labyrinth of sensationalism and unscriptural teaching. While we hold fast to the faith, we will not be deceived.

Weren't Ananias And Sapphira Demonized?

The Bible does not say that they were demon possessed, but that Satan filled their hearts to lie to the Holy Spirit (Acts 5:3). The difference is very clear to anyone who is not obsessed with demons.

Satan is the source of all temptation. He filled the hearts of those two church members, but there is no evidence that they were demon possessed. Ananias and Sapphira were carnal believers who listened to Satan instead of God. They did not resist the devil when he came to them with his evil suggestion, because of their greed.

This is the work of Satan: to tempt the people of God to fall into every sort of fleshly and worldly practice. What we need is not the casting out of demons, but the appropriation of the finished work of Christ on Calvary, and a consistent walk in the light.

Discerning Spirits Is A Gift For The Church.
Doesn't That Imply Demonization
Among Believers?

Some teachers argue this way, but we should notice that it is not called "the discerning of *evil* spirits" but simply "the discerning of spirits" (see I Cor. 12:10 KJV). The Revised Standard Version calls it "the ability to distinguish between spirits." Demons are not the only spirits that exist. Certainly angels are spirits too, and, at times, the Holy Spirit may dispense this gift that we might be aware of angelic presence (see II Kings 6:15-17). Beyond that, however, I believe we in the Body of Christ need to distinguish between demons and the expressions of our wicked and deceitful hearts, which we may legitimately call spirits (as in spirit of lust, jealousy, anger, deceit, etc.), so long as we understand that this is only a way of describing the enormous soul force of which each of us is capable when we want our own way.

These are the carnal spirits that keep us from inheriting the kingdom of God (Gal. 5:19-21), and it is among believers that this gift must function for the cleansing of the Body of Christ.

Can't The Spirit Be Truly Saved And Yet The Body Be Possessed?

That man has three parts—a body, soul, and spirit—has been an important premise for the doctrine of demons-in-believers. In his great chapter concerning the law of the spirit of life, Paul says, "If Christ is in you, though the body is dead because of sin, yet the spirit is alive because of righteousness" (Rom. 8:10). He explains how this death-life principle works. "For if you are living according to the flesh, you must die; but if by the Spirit you are putting to death the deeds of the body, you will live" (Rom. 8:13). The body is the locus of our sinful desires and in order to allow the life principle of the Spirit to dominate, we must mortify, or "put to death," the deeds of the body. By this process alone our bodies become temples of the Holy Spirit (I Cor. 6:19). "For ye are bought with a price: therefore glorify God in your body, and in your spirit, *which are God's*" (v. 20 KJV, italics mine).

The body belongs to God as well as the soul and the spirit. When God possesses one, He also takes control of the other. There is no scriptural basis for saying that one part of a man is saved while another remains in bondage to demons.

The folks who argue that believers can—indeed, that many do—have demons are really seeking some easier way to cope with that thorniest of problems, the flesh. The pathway of mortification is painful, but, because Christ's sacrifice has made it possible for us to become vessels of the Holy Spirit, it is possible as well as necessary.

Is It Dangerous For A Believer To Be In The Room Where Someone Is Being Delivered From Demons?

There is no cause to fear contact with people who are demon possessed. The one who is born again becomes the sanctuary of God in the Spirit (Eph. 2:22). Walk with the Lord in faith and obedience and you need have no fear of demons.

Are The Serious Problems With Immorality Symptoms Of Demon Possession?

It is easy to blame our sins on a demon because it relieves us from any personal responsibility. If you can persuade yourself that your undisciplined life is a result of demonic activity, you will never have to face up to the problem of trying to change what you are. All you have to do is be delivered from the demon of whatever is bothering you. But do not be deluded into trying to find a shortcut to spiritual victory through the casting out of demons. The works of the flesh are just what the Bible says they are: works of the flesh. Until you face this problem squarely and admit your need of the Holy Spirit's help, you will continue to suffer defeat, not at the hands of demons, but from your own willful desires.

Is There Such A Thing As A Sex Demon? Or A Demon Of Sloth?

Let me quote from the testimony of Jason Vinley who has published a small booklet under the title, *I Was Delivered From Deliverance.* I believe it will shed some light on this matter.

Several months ago I experienced what is today being called a deliverance. That is, I had brothers and sisters in Christ cast out evil spirits from me. I had all the manifestations that I was told I would have when demons were cast out of me. I spit up, coughed, shook, retched and screamed as each demon was named and commanded to leave.

As a young Christian I stumbled and fell many times. God in His love and mercy would always pick me up and strengthen me to walk. But I was always looking for a shortcut to holiness. Then I came across the teachings of certain ministers on demonology. They profess that it's not only possible for born-again believers to be in bondage to demons, but openly advocate that most Christians today are in dire need to have these evil spirits cast out of them.

These men knew the Lord, were Biblical scholars and their teachings were backed up with plenty of Scriptures. So I eagerly began to look for demon activity in my life. I was taught that if there are certain areas in your life in which you continually sin, such as anger or lust, you probably need a spirit of anger or lust cast out from you.

After my retching party, I was convinced that I had been set free. I listened to all the tapes and read all the books by these various ministers who teach on "deliverance" and I became eager to share this new truth with everybody.

It wasn't long after this, and much to my dismay, that I realized that I needed another deliverance. At first this bothered me, but I reasoned if I was still unclean, well, praise the Lord, let's go all the way this time. During my second deliverance I had about fifteen different demons cast out; everything from the spirit of suicide to the spirit of masturbation, no less. More coughing up, more yelling.

I praised God for cleansing me and proceeded to fast for three days.

During that fast, every time I belched I praised the Lord, believing that another demon spirit was coming out of me. That's what these ministers taught me. So I belched and praised the Lord for three days, and then I knew I was clean. At least for a while, I hoped.

I discovered another demon in my life: the demon of sloth. I found him while yawning in church on Sunday morning. I later discovered that this demon came into being by eating a large breakfast before going to church. I proceeded to cast this one out by myself, having become quite adroit by now.

Although this might seem ridiculous to you, I was reacting in the typical way many believers are doing today because of these erroneous teachings that are flooding the charismatic renewal. Every time affliction, temptation or sin would come crashing at my door, I would look for a demon rather than examine my life in the light of Scripture.

He concludes his testimony with this statement:

And those of you who have been erroneously led into deliverance sessions as I have, I simply ask you to stand on the Word and not your experience. Ask yourself this question: After the redemptive work of our Lord was completed on the cross, why is there not one recorded instance in the Bible of a Christian having, or being admonished to have a demon or evil spirit cast out of him? Study the Scriptures and God will give you the answer.

Why Do So Many Christians Believe That They Are Demon Possessed?

I think there may be two reasons for this. For one, most

of us hate to suffer and, since that is the Biblical formula for the solution to our problem (see I Pet. 4:1), we are eager to find some other way. The second reason is more a matter of mass psychology. Demons-in-believers was the latest fad in the charismatic movement and the pressure to get on the bandwagon was great. If you didn't get on you might be regarded as spiritually insensitive, or worse.

Have I Ever Been "Attacked" By Demons?

Between 1960 and 1973, my wife and I ministered in Brazil where over thirty million people practice the rites of spiritism, which often involve voluntary demon possession.* We have won many thousands of these spiritists to the Lord. This deeply angered their previous companions in spiritism. They often, I have since learned, performed the most vile and demonic rites against the one who was causing all the trouble. Thus I was the object of the worst kind of curses and imprecations.

I praise God that I have never once been conscious of a lack of protection from these curses. Aside from the normal times of discouragement, loneliness and those temptations that are common to all men, I cannot say that my lot is more difficult than that of anyone else. I believe that any attack on

---

*Spiritism promises that, if anyone wholeheartedly embraces it, they will possess great power and knowledge. They will be able to influence their surroundings as well as other people. They are deceived by a description of "good spirits" and "bad spirits" whom they come to know by name. They do not realize that all of these spirits are demonic, and thus willingly expose themselves to them. Finally they invite the so-called "good spirits" to possess them so that they might have maximum power and knowledge. That is what I mean by "voluntary" demon possession.

my life is Satanic rather than demonic. And as I resist him, he flees from me.

What Are The Similarities Between Being Filled With The Holy Spirit And Being Possessed By An Evil Spirit?

None whatever. The Spirit-filled person is a God-filled person. The Holy Spirit enters a believer at his invitation, and manifests Himself through that person in accordance with his obedience and faith.

Demon possession is different in every respect. Demons are of an inferior order than Satan, corresponding to angels in authority and function. They enter the body of an unbeliever without invitation and torment without permission or mercy.

Chapter V
DEMONS AND THE OCCULT

What Is Responsible For The Current Revival
Of Interest In Witchcraft, Astrology,
Psychic Phenomena, Etc?

We are very near to the Second Coming of the Lord. As it approaches, there will be increased activity in the realm of the spirit. On one hand, we are in the midst of the restoration of spiritual truths that have been hidden by centuries of tradition and church dogma. There is a worldwide outpouring of the Holy Spirit. Prophecies and visions are becoming a part of the life of faith.

Satan, on the other hand, knows his time is short, and he is not inactive. In colleges and suburban homes, spiritistic seances are taking place in every city in America. The newsstands are filled with occult literature. Witches, genies, and mediums are family fare on our television sets. This is all a part of the mystery of iniquity that will characterize the days just before the return of our Lord (II Thess. 2:7 KJV).

We can expect this explosion of the occult to increase as we approach the coming of the Lord. Satanic attacks on the mind and body will be greater. Evil spirits will be more and more active to capture the bodies of the unprotected. Our enemy does not intend to lose without a bitter fight, and the battleground is the heart, the soul, the mind, and the body of mankind.

What Is The Christian Church Doing About The Occult Revival?

The Christian church in America is partly responsible for the explosion of interest in the occult. The reasons are plain. In most Christian churches there is total ignorance of the power of the Holy Spirit to bring healing to body, soul, and spirit. The professional Christian ministry is simply not meeting the needs of church members. In his book on the occult, *Demons, Demons, Demons*, John P. Newport says, "The churches seem to be too rational, cold, impersonal and remote. This has helped to prepare the way for the occult sciences and the black arts."

If pastors withhold effective ministry from members, either through ignorance or fear, they should not blame them for seeking help elsewhere. Many church members are turning to magic and sorcery to find solutions to their urgent problems, and thus become ensnared in Satanic deception.

The only solution is to turn away from cold rationalism and to embrace the present-day outpouring of God's Holy Spirit. In every part of our nation, there is an awakening that can only be described as a sovereign move of the Spirit of God. Spiritual renewal is God's answer to the occult.

Is All Witchcraft And Sorcery The Result Of Demon Possession?

It will surprise many people to learn that idolatry and

sorcery are listed among the works of the flesh (Gal. 5:20). These things, which have often been considered purely Satanic in origin, are actually the result of man's carnal curiosity.

The prophet Samuel likened divination and idolatry to stubbornness and rebellion, which are acts of the flesh. "For rebellion is as the sin of divination, and insubordination is as iniquity and idolatry" (I Sam. 15:23). He also said that these things are practiced by the ungodly because they have rejected the word of the Lord. He said nothing about them being demon possessed.

Man has a tendency to regard as mystical things that originate in nothing higher than our fallen natures. We give names like telepathy, extrasensory perception, psychic phenomena, etc., to our spiritual wanderings and put the blame on the devil. In reality, man's lust for some kind of spiritual "kick" causes most of his involvement with the occult.

Certainly not every one who becomes involved with the various occult sciences is demon possessed. Nor is everyone who dabbles in sorcery and witchcraft filled with evil spirits. Those unhappy and often spiritually hungry people who involve themselves in such things live in the dangerous area of exposure to demonism. But neither the Scriptures, nor experience, bear out the theory that everybody who dabbles in the occult becomes, ipso facto, a demoniac.

There is, however, no doubt that many of these practices can lead to demon possession. The open worship of Satan is a direct appeal to the demonic, and those who engage themselves in these rites become easy prey to demons.

When A Person Is Hypnotized, Is He In Danger Of Demon Possession?

One thing a demon must do before he can enter a human

body is to reduce the power of the will to such an extent that he has freedom of entrance. This can happen in many ways. In Brazil, when a spiritistic medium calls on his *guia* (demonic guide to supernatural powers) to possess him, he will gulp large quantities of cheap liquor and inhale the smoke of strong cigars in order to get his own mind and will out of the way so that the spirit can more easily possess him.

In other forms of the occult sciences, trances and hypnotism are used to by-pass the human will and make room for the operation of what is sometimes described as the subconscious mind. When one voluntarily gives over his mind to the control of another person through hypnosis, he becomes highly vulnerable to the possibility of demonic entrance.

I know a woman who, when she was eleven years old, was hypnotized at a church social event. She remained in a trance for two hours and "came to" just as the ambulance was arriving. She was such a submissive subject to hypnotism that she was asked to "perform" on a number of subsequent occasions at the social gatherings of the church's young people. She told me years later that she had been plagued with fears and recurring visions since that night. She had become introspective and timid as a result of this dangerous brush with the occult, and her entire personality was warped with fears of the unknown.

Hypnotism is dangerous. It is used in many forms of occult worship. It opens the door of the mind to the spirit world. Those who enter this world find themselves subject to evil spirits who disguise themselves in all kinds of ways.

Hypnotism is becoming recognized as a medical tool for the treatment of both emotional and physical sicknesses. I would never submit myself to such therapy. The dangers are far too great. This is an area which I believe is forbidden to believers.

Does The Ouija Board Havw Anything To Do With Evil Spirits?

The Ouija board is not an innocent toy, but rather a tool of spiritualism. In appearance, it is just a game with letters and numbers. In reality, it is the kindergarten of the occult.

One girl in St. Johns, Arizona, shot and wounded her father when the Ouija board told her that her mother would marry another man. Millions of these "games" are sold annually. It is very popular among groups of young people. But invariably the party becomes more complicated as there is an urge to graduate from this kind of excitement. The next step is hypnotism, levitation, or spirit writing. The jump from these things to demonization is very short.

I recently asked a group of two hundred teenagers at a church youth camp how many had played with the Ouija board at social gatherings. The response was almost one hundred per cent in the affirmative. Many of them came to me with stories of levitation, telepathy, and psychic involvement that would have astounded their parents. Occult parlor games seem to be the norm in youth social gatherings, even among many church groups.

The same kind of curiosity that leads a person to the Ouija board will often lead him into more profound involvement with the occult that can only cause injury.

If you have a Ouija board in your home, destroy it.

Are Spiritualistic Mediums Demon Possessed?

Voluntary demon possession, under many different guises, is an integral part of the practice of spiritism and spiritualism around the world. It is basic to the receiving of supernatural knowledge and powers that are sought and used by the mediums.

One prominent Catholic scholar wrote that, in his thirty

years of the study of spiritism in Brazil, he had never met a medium who was not temporarily insane. This was his way of saying that the medium was possessed by another spirit than his own.

A medium in Brazil has written over one hundred books dealing with history, fiction, and spiritistic doctrine. He is a man of limited education and claims that all of these books were dictated to him by the spirits of wise men, long dead. He writes in a state of self-induced trance, wherein his pen moves across the paper without his cooperation.

I have listened to him explain how it was done, and in spite of his humble manner, I am sure that this spirit-writing is a demonic phenomenon. It is one of the lying wonders that is so very convincing and brings many people into bondage to demonic spirits. I see behind these psychic phenomena the cunningness of demons who seek to enslave the unprotected.

Believers who have been delivered from the bondage of spiritism affirm that they were set free from demonic powers which had been clothed in many disguises. One ex-medium explained to me that the darkness of her previous involvement with demons was only revealed when she came into the full light of the Gospel. She now recognizes that demon possession was the source of her occult powers.

When A Medium Contacts Spirits Of The Dead, Is He Actually Speaking To Demons?

In our church in Rio de Janeiro, there are two women who had dedicated most of their lives to Satan and his works. Georgina had been a spiritistic medium for thirty-three years, and Astrogilda for seventeen. In literally scores of hours of interviews over a ten-year period, they have helped me to understand the process of demonism.

It is interesting how Satan had rewarded those two faithful servants for their years of service. Astrogilda was a leper, and Georgina was dying of cancer of the blood when they came to our services and were healed by God's power.

They explained this matter of contacting the spirits of the dead. The vocabulary of spiritism describes demons in many ways, calling them "wise old ones," "disincarnate spirits of the dead," and "gods." After making sacrifices (sometimes of blood) to appease the spirits, they could make contact with them in order to obtain favors. There was never any doubt in their minds that they were dealing with demonic spirits of the underworld, who had varying degrees of power and influence.

Another member of our church in Brazil, Yvonne, was a medium for many years in what is called scientific spiritism. Its practitioners do not use blood or food sacrifices, but call on the spirits of the dead. It is what we would call spiritualism in America. For years she was deluded into thinking that she was actually speaking to the spirits of people who had died and passed into the spirit world. Today, with spiritual understanding, she realizes that she was involved with demons, and her many questions created by the manifestations of these spirits have now been answered in the light of God's Word.

In his book, *The Challenging Counterfeit*, Mr. Raphael Gasson gives a detailed look into the world of spiritualism in England. I recommend this book for a clear understanding of this type of spirit manifestation.

I should like to emphasize here that these three women mentioned above, all members of the New Life Pentecostal Church in Rio de Janeiro, accepted voluntary demon possession in order to exercise occult powers. But none of them had to be exorcised subsequent to her conversion. I have emphasized this because I want it clearly understood that the blood of Jesus Christ cleansed them from all sin.

A few months before this writing, Georgina celebrated her tenth year as a believer. Both Yvonne and Astrogilda have been saved for over eight years each. In spite of their many years of daily contact with demons, the work of cleansing was fully and finally done through the blood of Jesus at the moment of salvation. There was no demonic residue.

Is It Wrong To Attend A Seance Out Of Curiosity?

A Christian teenage boy attended a school party where a fifteen-year-old girl put herself into a trance and was levitated about two feet off the floor, to the great amusement of the twenty young people present. I advised him in the future to leave such parties with the explanation that he had no interest in such things. Seances are held regularly in homes all over our nation, and, sometimes, are the entertainment at parties. They should be avoided, whatever the cost in personal embarrassment, by those who wish to remain free of occult influence.

I will never forget the young girl, not yet in her teens, whose life was tormented day and night because of the deep psychic impressions made on her at one of these ad hoc spiritistic sessions. Satanic and demonic power can be very convincing. The Bible speaks of lying wonders as part of the wickedness that will involve those who do not embrace the truth of the Gospel (II Thess. 2:9-10).

It is as wrong to attend a seance out of curiosity as it is to steal just to see how it feels. There can be no fellowship between good and evil, between light and darkness.

When A Christian Becomes Involved In The Occult, Can He Become Demon Possessed?

I find it difficult to imagine that a believer who is walking in obedience to God would become involved in the occult. But many churchgoers, having received little or no spiritual food in their churches, have begun in desperation to dabble in the occult sciences and psychic phenomena.

Those who do become involved in the occult are voluntarily exposing themselves to the possibility of demonization. The presence of the Holy Spirit in such a believer's life will protect him. Normally He will sound a loud warning to His servant who is responsible to hear it and repent. If he doesn't hear it, he'd better find out why—he should ask God to show him what in his life is making him so deaf to His voice.

I know of a woman who belonged to an evangelical church where there was no faith for healing and whose daughter was ill. A neighbor invited her to take her afflicted daughter to a spiritistic meeting. After many weeks, the girl became well. When the mother wanted to return to her church, the daughter said, "But mother, I can't leave. The spirits won't let me go."

Those who seek help, or guidance, or favors of any kind in the occult sciences must realize that the powers they invoke are demonic. There is a high price to be paid when demons grant favors: it is bondage to evil spirits. Nothing you need is worth such a price.

If You Have Been Exposed To The Occult, Is There A Danger That You May Become Demon Possessed?

There is a great difference between exposure and involvement. By exposure, I understand some sort of contact with spiritualism like visiting a seance or maintaining a friendship with someone who is involved in the occult.

Let me give you my personal testimony in this regard.

In the beginning of my ministry in Rio de Janeiro, I became aware that the strange stories that I was hearing about spiritism were attributable to demonic spirits. Although I had witnessed demon possession in my evangelistic ministry in the Orient and Europe, I did not clearly understand how these things worked. At first, I thought it was mental illness of some kind. I had to be sure.

So I attended a number of spiritistic ceremonies in 1961. I witnessed their demonic baptisms under the waterfalls in the northern state of Bahia. I listened to the incantations to evil spirits. I watched mediums perform healings through demonic power. I saw an initiation rite in which twelve-year-old girls begged evil spirits to possess their bodies. With each experience, my understanding of demonism grew. I began to understand the conditions under which evil spirits can function. I understood the work of a demon in the human body. The more I saw, the more compassionate I became for demoniacs.

While doing this, I was never conscious of being "attacked" by evil spirits. It was uncomfortable in those places. I was intensely aware that I should not remain in them beyond the point of my own necessary education. Since that time I have never visited them again.

The blood-washed believer is protected wherever he goes. I would not recommend that anyone expose himself to the occult. But if for any reason there is exposure, I am convinced that the power of God is greater than the powers of darkness. There is no reason to fear that a demon is going to jump on you and overcome you. It is we who are the overcomers.

If You Have Been Involved In The Occult Before Salvation, Do You Need To Have Demons Cast Out Of You?

I have already dealt with this briefly, but let me quote again from the illuminating testimony of Mr. Jason Vinley:

I was told by the "deliverance ministers" of the many

82

and varied ways in which evil spirits could get inside you to cause bondage, but the most common way for demons to enter was through involvement with the occult, even if that involvement was before you were saved. When I heard that, I was hooked for sure. Before I had become a Christian I wound myself through all sorts of occult trips searching for God. I sought Him in astrology and drugs. In my darkness I rummaged through yoga, reincarnation and hypnosis looking for Him. I delved into parapsychology, spiritism and divination.

When I finally did find my Lord and Savior I believed that I was delivered from all my previous bondage. But now these teachers convinced me that the source of my problem was demonic subjection because of these years of darkness, even though I did it in ignorance.

Mr. Vinley finally came to realize that he whom the Son sets free is free indeed. By hard experience he learned that his first impression had been correct. When he found Jesus as Lord and Savior, he was delivered from all previous bondage.

I wrote a book in Portuguese entitled, *Mother of Saints*. It is the biography of Georgina Aragao dos Santos (mentioned in a previous question), who was baptized in the blood of animals at the age of fifteen, and who for thirty-three years was a medium in *Candomble* (low-spiritism) in the cities of Salvador and Rio de Janeiro.

Georgina was involved in every type of demonic ritual, from blood sacrifice to divination. She was a medium, a fortune teller, and a practitioner of both white and black magic. At her ordination as a priestess, she became possessed by a demon spirit whose name she knew and whose powers she invoked daily. This voluntary demonization gave her occult powers, and her life was entirely dedicated to their use.

Georgina was dying of leukemia when she came to a midweek service in our church. She was both healed and saved; saved both from her sins and from the demonic power of her blood oaths. If ever there was a person who might have a "demonic residue" after salvation, it was Georgina.

In the preparation for this book, I talked with Georgina about the false doctrine of demons-in-believers. I told her about the theory that demonic residue exists in the lives of those who had practiced the occult before their salvation. Her response was instantaneous. "Pastor Roberto, that is one of the biggest lies that the devil ever told. How could any real Christian ever believe such a thing?" A good question.

I never cast a demon out of Georgina. It wasn't necessary. The expulsive power of salvation through the blood of Christ completely destroyed the influence of demons over her life. That happened in 1962. I waited for six years to tell her story.

Now, after more than a dozen years, she rarely misses a worship service. She is a Spirit-filled witness to the delivering power of God through simple faith in Jesus Christ.

Chapter VI
Deliverance from Demon Possession

Who Has The Authority
To Cast Out A Demon?

According to Jesus, anyone who believes can cast out an evil spirit. "And these signs will accompany those who have believed: in My name they will cast out demons" (Mark 16:17).

On one occasion Jesus called the twelve disciples together and gave them power and authority over all demons (Luke 9:1). Later, He gave the same power to seventy disciples who returned and reported that the demons were subject to them in His name (Luke 10:1,17).

In one dramatic case, some unbelieving Jewish exorcists, the Sons of Sceva, were attempting to cast out devils "in the name of Jesus whom Paul preaches." The evil spirits recognized their lack of authority and leapt on them, overpowering them. The would-be exorcists fled from the scene naked and wounded (Acts 19:13-16).

The problem here was lack of authority and protection. Those men were not believers in Jesus Christ even though they used the correct formula. They had no real protection against the demons.

It is not necessary to be an ordained minister of the Gospel in order to cast out demons. The authority and gifts necessary for this ministry are available to all believers (I Cor. 12:7-10). Even as light casts out darkness, so the power of God is greater than the power of Satan. Any believer under the New Covenant can exercise this power under the anointing of the Holy Spirit.

Should A New Christian Cast Out Demons?

Nothing in the Bible indicates that a new believer has any less authority to use the name of Jesus than one who has walked with the Lord for many years. However, because of the responsibilities involved in the ministry of casting out demons, it would seem only prudent to wait for a clear understanding of your position in Christ before attempting to cast out evil spirits. Paul warned Timothy that there are certain responsibilities that should not be given to a new convert (I Tim. 3:6).

This is not work for one who is a novice, immature, or fearful. It is a job for the mature child of God who knows his position and can speak with full authority in the face of demonic challenge.

When Facing A Demon-Possessed Person, What Is The Responsibility Of A Layman?

It is a mistake to think that only apostles, prophets, evangelists, pastors or teachers have the authority to cast out demons. People who occupy those offices are responsible for the doctrine, discipline, and direction of the Church. They have been given to us for the perfecting of the saints, for the work of the ministry, and for the edifying of the Body of Christ (Eph. 4:12 KJV).

When face to face with a demonized person, a layman has the same responsibility as a minister. He should cast out the demon in the name of Jesus. The only qualifications one needs to do this is a knowledge of Christ as Lord, and an understanding of the power of the name of Jesus (Mark 16:17).

How Does One Pray
For A Demon-Possessed Person?

Prayer, except for oneself as the exorcist, is ineffective for the expulsion of demons. Rather, you must speak to the evil spirit in the authority of the name of Jesus.

Mark records the story of an unclean spirit whom Jesus cast out. You will remember that Jesus spoke directly to the demon, saying, "You deaf and dumb spirit, I command you, come out of him and do not enter him again" (Mark 9:25).

Is Prayer Unnecessary
In Casting Out Demons?

Not at all. When the disciples asked the Lord why they could not cast out the spirit, He replied, "This kind cannot come out by anything but prayer" (Mark 9:27-29). Jesus did not pray for the young demoniac, but He had prepared Himself through prayer to the Father in order to be equipped for this ministry.

The King James version of Matthew 17:21 indicates that the preparation for casting out demons is both prayer and fasting. It is folly to face demonic powers without personal preparation. But at the moment when the demon is cast out, the word of authority in the name of Jesus is the only power he will obey. In other words, you must do your praying *before* you start casting out demons.

How Do You Know When Fasting Is Required Before Casting Out A Demon?

Matthew 17:14-21 tells the story of the disciples who were helpless to cast out a demon. When the disciples asked Jesus why, Jesus replied, "This kind goeth not out but by prayer and fasting" (KJV).

Many translations, including the New American Standard Bible, omit this verse entirely and claim that the most reliable manuscripts do not include it. The New Scofield Reference Edition of the Bible, in a marginal note, says that some reliable manuscripts omit verse twenty-one.

Whether or not Jesus made this statement is not really the issue. Our preparation for any spiritual exercise should be in proportion to the challenge that we will face. The man who walks to work doesn't have to be in the same physical condition as the one who runs a race.

In the first part of this book I recounted the case of Clarita Villenueva. Before Pastor Lester Sumrall faced the demons who possessed Clarita, he prepared himself with fasting and prayer. I shared with him in this experience. Mr. Sumrall knew that he would face the fury of demonic power as well as the scorn of the world press, and felt that he needed the added spiritual vigor that comes through fasting before the Lord.

In most of the cases where demoniacs have been brought to me, it was not possible to go away and fast and pray before confronting the demonic power. I can remember only three times in over twenty years when I felt that I should prepare myself to cast out demons by fasting.

In the bibliography at the end of this book I include two books that have helped me to understand the benefits of fasting. I recommend them for further study on this subject.

How Does One Cast Out A Demon?

Jesus gave us the formula: "And these signs will accompany those who have believed: in My name they will cast out demons" (Mark 16:17).

At Philippi, when Paul was disturbed by the slave girl who had a spirit of divination, he said to the spirit, "I command you in the name of Jesus Christ to come out of her" (Acts 16:17-18).

Authority rests in the name of Jesus because, as Isaiah said, His name would be called Mighty God (Is. 9:6). God has given the same authority to the name of Jesus that He gave to the person of Jesus. "And Jesus came up and spoke to them, saying, 'All authority has been given to Me in heaven and on earth' " (Matt. 28:18).

When you speak in the name of Jesus, you are speaking with the authority of His person. When you cast out demons in the name of Jesus they cannot resist. Evil spirits recognized the Lord when He ministered here on earth; they knew Him and feared him. Demons know and recognize the authority of His name today, and are unable to resist it when it is announced in the power of the Holy Spirit.

Shoule You Cast Out Demons
With The Laying On Of Hands?

In the Bible, there is no record where demons were ever cast out through the laying on of hands.

In every instance where the laying on of hands was practiced, whether it was for the healing of the sick (Luke 4:40), the ordination of ministries (Acts 13:3), the infilling of the Holy Spirit (Acts 8:17), or the impartation of spiritual gifts (I Tim. 4:14), it was always to bestow blessing.

Since it is inappropriate to bless demons, they should not be exorcised with the laying on of hands. This does not mean that you may not touch someone who is under demonic attack. On many occasions I have had to defend myself against attack by a demoniac. One very frightening experience happened in the city of Sao Paulo, Brazil, when a woman tried to strangle me when I began to expel the evil spirit who possessed her. She had to be restrained while I challenged and cast out the demon.

When Jesus delivered the daughter of Abraham from her eighteen years of bondage by a spirit of infirmity, He first cast out the demon, and then, following her deliverance, laid His hands on her for the healing of her deformity (Luke 13:11-13). The Lord ministered healing to her through the laying on of hands only after she had been set free from the evil spirit.

This is one point on which I was ignorant for many years. I had seen men cast out demons with the laying on of hands, and so, in the beginning of my ministry, I did what I had learned. But I was always disturbed by the wrestling matches which ensued. When I finally realized that the name of Jesus alone was power enough to cast out demons, it was a great relief to me.

Jesus clearly defined the distinction between healing the sick and setting demoniacs free: "And these signs will accompany those who have believed: in My name they will *cast out* demons; they will *lay hands on* the sick, and they will recover" (Mark 16:17-18, italics mine).

What Must Be Done Before A Demon Can Be Cast Out?

The principal tool of demons is secrecy. They will masquerade in all kinds of disguises. They are expert liars and give themselves the most fantastic names, anything to avoid exposure.

Often, when challenged, a demon will simply leave the body of a demoniac in order to avoid exposure and expulsion. Or he may remain mute and even afflict his victim with dumbness in order to hide. But he must respond to the name of Jesus.

The woman possessed by demons from the legion of blood, mentioned earlier, suffered from lockjaw every time she was attacked by the evil spirits. At my first encounter, I commanded the demons to speak in the name of Jesus. Her jaw dropped open instantly. Until that moment, the evil spirit had successfully hidden himself for fifteen years.

This is why I require a demon to speak. Most of what he says will be untrue, but, when he speaks, he has exposed his presence. In most cases the step between exposure and expulsion is very short.

Is Speaking With Demons Really Necessary?

While not every case of exorcism in Scripture indicates dialogue with a demon, it is commonplace in several instances. For the reasons I just explained, I have found this a very important part of the deliverance process.

Both experience and the gift of discernment are very important. Often, evil spirits will threaten to do terrible things if they are cast out. Demons have told me, on countless occasions, that they would "get me," or come back and destroy the person who was being delivered. The inexperienced might be intimidated, and only the discerning of spirits, coupled with calm authority in the name of Jesus, can bring the situation into focus and under control.

Can You Tell If A Person Is Demon Possessed By Asking Him If He Believes In Jesus?

I don't suppose there is anyone who "believes in Jesus" more than a demon. In the instance of the Jewish exorcists, an evil spirit said, "I recognize Jesus" (Acts 19:15). Demons know that it is the Lord Jesus who will cause their final destruction. "And behold, they cried out, saying, 'What do we have to do with You, Son of God? Have you come here to torment us *before the time?*' " (Matt. 8:29, italics mine).

Demons believe in Jesus in the sense that they know who He is, and they are painfully aware of His supreme authority over them. If, however, you ask a person who is under demonic control whether or not Jesus Christ is his Lord, you will get a different answer. No demon will acknowledge that Jesus is Lord.

Can Anyone Cast Out A Demon By Using The Phrase, "In The Name Of Jesus"?

Demons do not fear the *sound* of the name of Jesus, but the *authority* of that name. No magical powers attend the repetition of Jesus' name and it cannot be used as an incantation. This is perfectly illustrated by the story in Acts 19:13-16, the sons of Sceva who tried to cast out demons in the name of Jesus, but who had to flee wounded and naked. The power of God did not accompany the use of the name spoken by unbelievers.

C.S. Lovett says it this way: "When Christ invites us to do mighty things in His name, He is not giving us a formula, but authority. It is a matter of moving in power, not reciting magical words."

The successful use of the name of Jesus depends on whether or not the user is one who has already believed in Christ. "And these signs will accompany those *who have believed*" (Mark 16:17, italics mine).

Must Demons Obey A Believer When He Uses The Name Of Jesus?

That depends on what we mean by "obey." Our authority over demons is limited, in the sense that we cannot destroy them. We cannot send them to the pit, nor control all of their future actions.

"When the unclean spirit goes out of a man, it passes through waterless places seeking rest, and not finding any, it says, 'I will return to my house from which I came.' And when it comes, it finds it swept and put in order. Then it goes and takes along seven other spirits more evil than itself, and they go in and live there; and the last state of that man becomes worse than the first" (Luke 11:24-26).

In this description of the comings and goings of a demon, Jesus shows that, when an evil spirit has left, or has been cast out, the only guarantee against future possession is whether or not the "house" (the body of the demoniac) has been occupied by one more powerful: the Spirit of God.

That's why I spend a lot of time with the person who has just been delivered, explaining the profound dangers of an unprotected life. I urge the ex-demoniac to recognize the claims of Christ and give him solemn warning that unless he receives Jesus as his Lord, he will be vulnerable to future demonic attacks.

Even when there has been a titanic struggle, and the newly-delivered individual is exhausted, it is vitally important not to leave him ignorant that Jesus wants to become his Savior and protector. No one should attempt to cast out a demon who is not also prepared to minister the Gospel with great patience and conviction to the one whose house has been swept clean. You must not leave a vacuum.

Can We Bind And Destroy Demons?

We have been given the authority to bind demons, but not to destroy them. By "binding" we mean restraint. There appears to be no other sense in which we can bind evil spirits. Jesus bound a demon when He said, "You deaf and dumb spirit, I command you, come out of him and *do not enter him again*" (Mark 9:25, italics mine).

When Jesus delivered the demoniac of Gadara (Matt.

8:28-34), the demons begged to be sent into a herd of swine, presumably to avoid those waterless places. Jesus did not destroy demons, and He has not given us authority to do it. I am disturbed by someone who tries to consign demons to "the pit." They will be dealt with in accordance with Bible prophecy (Matt. 25:41).

As demon possession increases all over the world, those who exorcise must understand the nature and the limits of their authority. When we go beyond the limits of scriptural authority we bring confusion.

Is It Necessary To "Plead The Blood" Of Jesus Before Casting Out A Demon?

If the person who casts out demons is living in spiritual victory, he need not "plead the blood" since that has reference to our sin. If he is not walking with the Lord because of unconfessed sin, he has no business trying to cast out evil spirits.

Special phrases as a sort of "spiritual incantation" to ward off the evil spirit are needless. Our protection against demons is constant and complete through Christ our defender.

How Do Demons Act When They Are Cast Out?

In one instance, when Jesus delivered a boy, "He rebuked the unclean spirit, saying to it, 'You deaf and dumb spirit, I command you, come out of him and do not enter him again.' And after crying out and throwing him into terrible convulsions, it came out; and the boy became so much like a corpse that most of them said, 'He is dead' " (Mark 9:25-26).

I can hardly remember a single case where the evil spirit left quietly, even though he knew that he was powerless to remain in the face of the authority of Jesus' name. When his authority to possess a human body is being challenged, a demon may cause the demoniac to writhe on the floor like a snake, to go into violent convulsions, or even to inflict bodily harm on himself.

In the case of Astrea and the "legion of blood," the fifth and final encounter with the demon was so dramatic that the family was certain that Astrea was dead when she slumped to the floor after being freed from demonic bondage. In fact, she was completely exhausted.

No two exorcisms are exactly alike. But most often there is a violent upheaval just before complete deliverance, depending largely on how long the demon had been "in residence."

Must One Vomit Demons When They Are Cast Out?

Jason Vinley says his "retching party" resulted from preconditioning his mind by those who taught that he was filled with many evil spirits and told him to vomit them up. Doctor Robert C. Frost, author of *Aglow with the Spirit*, wrote to me, "I have sometimes wondered if some 'mass deliverance' sessions have not been psychologically induced in part or perhaps even provided Satan the stage upon which he can draw attention to himself."

It is impossible to say exactly what will happen in any given instance of exorcism. Yet some groups come to a session with paper towels or air-sickness bags into which they plan to spit demons. I have seen demoniacs foam at the mouth during their torment, but this was not because they were taught to vomit up a demon.

No reference in the Bible instructs a demoniac to spit up a demon. If this were merely foolishness, it could be tolerated. But it is worse than that. It is a false doctrine that brings the people of God into bondage.

Where Do Demons Go
When They Are Cast Out?

The Bible tells us that when an evil spirit leaves a man it goes into the waterless places, seeking rest, but does not find it (Matt. 12:43). Outside of the physical world that we can see and touch, there is a spirit world. Paul defines Satan as being "the prince of the power of the air" (Eph. 2:2). It is in this realm of spiritual darkness where demons dwell.

When demons are cast out, they should be sent to the arid, waterless places of the earth. We have no authority to cast them into hell, nor to destroy them. When dispossessed of a human body, they return to the darkness from which they emerged to torment.

Does This Mean That Demons Are Not
Destroyed When Their Power
To Possess Is Broken?

Demons are not subject to the laws of birth and death. The spirits who possess people today are the same ones who possessed other people in Jesus' day. They inspired the immorality of Sodom and Pompeii. They provoked the atrocities of Attila and Hitler.

Demons have existed since they fell from angelhood with Lucifer in his rebellion. They were cast to the earth where they will function until Jesus casts them into the eternal fire prepared for their torment.

What Do You Do When You Command
A Demon To Go And He Doesn't?

In the "legion of blood" case, I had to face Astrea's demons five times before they left for good. The first four times they left, but their power was not broken. We were in a life and death struggle against demons who had been in

96

residence for fifteen years. After the fifth encounter, everyone there knew the deliverance was complete.

There have been times when the struggle for deliverance became so great that the demoniac's life was endangered, and I decided to discontinue the battle for a while. In cases like this, it is no lack of faith to come back the following day and try again. In each succeeding encounter, the demon's resolve weakens until he finally decides to leave for good.

Do You Always Have Success In Casting Out Demons?

Such cases of "delayed deliverance" might indicate a lack of authority, but I don't think so. When Lester Sumrall grappled three different times with "The Thing" that possessed Clarita, none of us who watched could doubt that Jesus' name was supreme.

These cases of prolonged struggle are, however, rare. Most of the time demons leave at the first command. Sometimes sincere believers try to cast out demons, but without success. Generally that is because they are unsure of their authority. Demons can detect this and will not obey the uncertain challenge. When that happens, find someone who can see the problem and speak with authority.

How Do You Feel When You Have Cast Out A Demon?

It is easy to imagine that successful exorcism could give one a pretty heady feeling, but the opposite is true. I have never recognized my helplessness more clearly than when I've stood before a demoniac in torment. It is not a time to speak glibly of past successes. Demons are not impressed by our experience. It may be possible to preach without any unusual anointing, or to teach things we've taught before, or even to pray for the sick as a matter of routine. But no one can cast out a demon without the power of Almighty God. Every time a victory has come I've felt only relieved and thankful that the King had once again conquered the forces of darkness.

What Gifts Of The Spirit Are Needed To Cast Out Demons?

There is no specific gift called, "the casting out of demons." Basically, one needs the gift of the discerning of spirits. The New American Standard Bible calls it "the distinguishing of spirits" (I Cor. 12:10). There is no way to be sure that someone is demon possessed without it since symptoms cannot guarantee a correct diagnosis.

Once you have decided that a person is demonized you may need the gift of faith (I Cor. 12:9). Fighting demons has challenged my faith and, in turn, given me new understanding of Jesus' power.

There were times when the struggle was so great that I was sure nothing short of the gift of miracles would effect the deliverance. But we mustn't lose sight of the simple formula Jesus gave us for this work: "In My name they will cast out demons" (Mark 16:17).

Is Discerning Spirits Used Only To Determine If Someone Is Demon Possessed?

I've discussed this question earlier in a different setting (see p. ms. 59). Here I want to reemphasize that this gift will reveal the nature of one's spirit, whether it be of God, of demons, or of the flesh. To uncover a carnal spirit, a deceitful spirit, or a jealous spirit, even when they might be disguised by tears and soft words, would prevent great destruction to the work of the Lord and violence to the Body of Christ. These deceitful, jealous and factious spirits are not demons but expressions of our souls when not submitted to the Spirit of God.

If we could recognize the bitterness and self-seeking that lie beneath so many conflicts, how much easier it would be to end them and the problems they produce within the Body of Christ. I can think of many situations when personal tragedy could have been avoided had someone been courageous enough to say what he discerned by the Holy Spirit.

How often has some sinful situation been exposed and someone asked, "Why didn't somebody see this before now?" The answer is that we have used the gift of discernment to unmask demons, but have failed to use it to unmask the insincere, reveal the deceitful, and expose the unrighteous in time for discipline and restitution.

How Does The Discerning Of Spirits Work In Relation To The Ministry Of Casting Out Demons?

This question was asked among a group of ministers who were dealing with "borderline" cases where there seemed to be demonic powers present, and where the individual had been involved with the occult sciences. They were wisely reluctant to cast out demons until they were sure demons actually possessed the disturbed people who came for counseling.

I was once called by a fellow-minister to counsel a young woman who had attended a witch's coven to get advice about her problem with her husband. She had been a church member, but had drifted away, become divorced, and now was returning to my friend for help. He had had little experience with witchcraft and asked me to talk with the woman to see if she was demonized or only emotionally disturbed by her contact with the occult.

She told me about the ceremony in which she had participated and about her constant nervousness, uncontrolled weeping and occasional violent behavior since then. I asked the Holy Spirit to let me see the truth behind her words.

I began to see that she had indeed exposed herself to demons on two occasions. It had frightened her deeply and she had a guilty conscience. But she was not possessed by an evil spirit. I told her what I had discerned, and we prayed in the name of Jesus for her forgiveness and deliverance from the depression and violence. From that day she became a radiant Christian with no recurrence of the emotional distress.

The gift of discerning spirits works as a "knowing" which can only be explained in terms of the indwelling Spirit who reveals the truth necessary to solve the problem.

Can Children Be Demon Possessed?

Yes. In the case of the boy who had a deaf and dumb spirit, Jesus asked the father how long he had had it. The father replied, "From childhood" (Mark 9:21). The woman in Brazil who was demonized because of her blasphemous imitation of prophecy told me she had been possessed from the time she was nine years old.

What Do You Do For A Person After He Has Been Delivered From Possession?

When a demon is cast out, the victim is usually exhausted from the struggle, but he must understand what has happened and that Jesus is his only protection against subsequent demon possession. (See p. ms. 88).

In the case of Clarita Villenueva, the evil spirits returned many times, until she repeated the sinner's prayer and received the protection of the blood of Christ. The "house" was then filled with the forgiveness and love of God, and the demons could not re-enter.

I know two people who were delivered from demons and later returned to their sins. They each became demon possessed more violently and implacably than before.

The person who casts out a demon must evangelize the victim immediately. If he is reluctant to repent, warning in Matthew 12:43-45 should be read and explained.

Can A Demoniac Exorcise Himself?

Demons often temporarily leave a demoniac in full control of his mind and body (Luke 11:24). When a demoniac is under attack, he does not know what is happening to him. He may be told that he has "spells" or epilepsy. Generally their families don't understand the problem. Only rarely will a medical doctor or psychiatrist diagnose it as demon possession.

Demonized people are commonly unaware of the nature of their problem, and they usually go to the wrong places to find help. If one were aware of the demonic source of his trouble, he could, during a temporary absence of his tormentor, call upon the Lord to have mercy upon him and repent. This would change those conditions which allowed the demon to enter him in the first place. And he would be free from demonic power, because the superior power of God's light had entered to preclude its re-entrance.

Only under these circumstances could a demoniac be delivered without an exorcist.

If A Friend Or Member Of The Family Is Demon Possessed What Should One Do?

First, ask the Lord to give you discernment so that you can discover exactly what the problem is. If you find he is demon possessed, you should command the evil spirit to leave in the name of Jesus. Study the Bible to learn how demons are subject to Jesus. If you are unsure of your authority, or nervous about facing demonic power, seek out someone with experience and ask for their advice and help.

But please do not go around indiscriminately "discerning" demons in believers and exorcising them.

How Does One Know Whether Or Not He Can Cast Out Demons?

Someone asked me how you can know you have received the gifts of healing. I replied that the best way was to pray for the sick. I was not being facetious. The best way to find out if God will honor you when you use the name of His Son, is to use it against demons. You will soon discover how great is your faith. As I said earlier, every true believer has this authority if he will use it.

Should You Ever Tell A Person That He Is Demon Possessed?

Normally, if a person is possessed, you'll not be able to talk to him. But, if, as would rarely happen, you meet a demoniac during the temporary absence of his demon, you should speak urgently to him about his need for Christ. Under these circumstances it would be appropriate to tell him you have discerned that he is demonized.

However, that's not the problem. Today there are people all over this country telling Christians en masse that they certainly have demons. They claim that almost all sickness is actually demon possession and they pray for the sick by exorcising them. I know of one woman who died as the result of such an ordeal. She was a faithful Christian and yet was told that her sickness was caused by demons who inhabited her. Her friends told me she died of fear.

Let's stop telling Christians they are demonized and begin using the gift of discerning spirits carefully.

Should We Hunt Out Demon-Possessed People To Set Them Free?

No. Jesus never went about looking for demon-possessed people. "And when evening had come, they *brought* to Him many who were demon possessed; and He cast out the spirits with a word, and healed all who were ill" (Matt. 8:16, italics mine). When Paul cast the demon out of the slave-girl, it was because she persistently followed him through the streets and kept crying out (Acts 16:16-17).

When Jesus commissioned the Twelve, He gave them power and authority over all demons and "sent them out to proclaim the kingdom of God, and to perform healing" (Luke 9:1-2). They were told to preach the Gospel and to heal the sick, but at no time were they told to look for demon-possessed people. However, when the disciples did encounter demoniacs, they had authority to deliver them through the name of Jesus (Luke 10:17).

BIBLIOGRAPHY

Adolph, Paul E., *Release from Tension*. Chicago, Moody Press, 1956.

Basham, Don W., *Can a Christian Have a Demon?* Monroeville, Penna., Whitaker Books, 1971.

————*Deliver Us from Evil*. Washington Depot, Conn., Chosen Books, 1972.

Beall, James Lee, *Rise to Newness of Life*. Detroit, Mich., Evangel Press, 1974.

————*The Adventure of Fasting*. Old Tappan, N.J., Fleming H. Revell Co., 1974.

Gasson, Raphael, *The Challenging Counterfeit*. Plainfield, N.J., Logos International, 1966.

Huegel, F.J., *That Old Serpent—the Devil*. Grand Rapids, Mich., Zondervan Publishing House, 1954.

Lovett, C.S., *Dealing with the Devil*. Baldwin Park, Calif., Personal Christianity, 1967.

McMillen, S.I., *None of These Diseases*. Westwood, N.J., Fleming H. Revell, 1967.

Meade, Russell J., *Victory over Demonism Today*. Wheaton, Ill., Christian Life Publications, 1962.

Munsey, Grace, *Casting out Spirits God's Way*. 324 S.J. St., Lake Worth, Fla.

Newport, John P., *Demons, Demons, Demons*. Nashville, Tenn., Broadman Press, 1972.

Prince, Derek, *Expelling Demons*. Box 306, Ft. Lauderdale, Fla.

Unger, Merrill F., *Demons in the World Today*. Wheaton, Ill., Tyndale House, 1971.

Vinley, Jason, *I Was Delivered from Deliverance*. 1705 N. Allendale Ave., Sarasota, Fla.

Wallis, Arthur, *God's Chosen Fast*. Fort Washington, Penn., Christian Literature Crusade, 1968.